C000132272

Holistic Website Planning

Positioning your website at the centre of your digital transformation

Andrew Armitage

R^ethink

First published in Great Britain in 2021
by Rethink Press (www.rethinkpress.com)

© Copyright Andrew Armitage

All rights reserved. No part of this publication may be reproduced, stored in or introduced into a retrieval system, or transmitted, in any form, or by any means (electronic, mechanical, photocopying, recording or otherwise) without the prior written permission of the publisher.

The right of Andrew Armitage to be identified as the author of this work has been asserted by him in accordance with the Copyright, Designs and Patents Act 1988.

This book is sold subject to the condition that it shall not, by way of trade or otherwise, be lent, resold, hired out, or otherwise circulated without the publisher's prior consent in any form of binding or cover other than that in which it is published and without a similar condition including this condition being imposed on the subsequent purchaser.

*For my dad, who inspired me to start my own business,
and my daughters, Sophie and Ellie, who may
one day start their own*

Contents

Introduction

For as long as I can remember, I've had a love for technology. When the World Wide Web was becoming established in 1989, I was a curious eleven-year-old. Over the following years, CD-ROMs from early internet service providers like Netscape, AOL and CompuServe would drop through the door on an almost daily basis, and I would find myself running a telephone extension line from my parents' bedroom to a US Robotics 56k modem sitting on top of a giant tower computer. By the mid-nineties, I'd registered my first domain name and was hosting a website using a service called GeoCities.

Several years later, while studying for my Business Studies degree, I learned to write code, and during a work placement year with a global oil giant, I was handed a copy of Microsoft FrontPage 98 and told to build an intranet that would enable the much-aspired-to paperless office. Needless to say, this goal was far too ambitious for a placement student to achieve alone. I've still yet to see a paperless office, but it was obvious the potential was huge.

Fast forward twenty years and 'digital' is central to how we live, communicate, find information and seek entertainment. I started writing this book in 2019, and a few months later, the world was under lockdown during the COVID-19 pandemic. In that time, most people saw first-hand how digital technology and eCommerce helped to maintain a functional society and how the businesses that built their strategy with an emphasis on digital would be best placed to emerge strongest from the crisis. Digital was already well ingrained in our society, but COVID-19 accelerated changes in behaviour from both businesses and consumers that left any company with gaps in their approach to digital at serious risk of being left behind.

Why this book?

Businesses that can provide digital experiences, products and communities have been able to scale up, trade internationally and, in exceptional cases, allow their founders to achieve the dream of making money while they sleep. Yet despite 'the web' maturing over time and there being a plethora of free how-to guides, videos, blog posts and podcasts, I still hear plenty of stories from people who haven't seen the results they were hoping for from their website.

Your website sits at the centre of your digital activity and will almost always be the main authority for your business online. Unlike social media platforms, your website is something you own and control; although search engines can hugely influence how people find you online, your website provides a blank canvas for how you want to be seen and what you want to be known for. It is so important to your overall digital presence and performance; you cannot afford to get it wrong.

In this book, I'm going to share the ingredients you need to plan a successful website that can transform the future of your business. Websites don't work in isolation, though, so we'll be working through a methodology called **Go the DISTANCE** that explores everything you'll need to consider for your website to have a positive impact on your business. With some joined-up thinking, your website will become one of your best-performing assets sitting at the heart of your digital ecosystem, integrating with technology across the business, and driven by strategic thinking and a customer-centric focus.

This book doesn't 'explain' digital marketing. I'm not going to talk about the best funnel-building tools or how to optimise your Facebook ads; instead, I'll show you everything you need to consider before you start your next website project. Having read this book, you'll be able to write a detailed brief, set a budget and put together a project team to create a site that supports your strategy, internal processes and the needs of your customers, setting you on a path to building a great digital business.

While the Go the DISTANCE methodology will work for any business, the focus of this book is on existing companies whose founders/leaders have realised their digital activity overall (not just their website) could perform better for them. Your website may sit at the centre of your digital ecosystem, but it needs systems and processes to work behind it to enable scale and growth.

In the twelve years I've been running my digital agency, I've led hundreds of website projects, many of which have presented a series of common challenges that inhibit the way a project progresses and its likelihood of success once it's launched. As my team and I refined our process to overcome these obstacles, we observed eight key elements that required detailed consideration (and often guidance) before we could be confident that the new website would deliver on a client's aspirations. These elements form the basis of the model called Go the DISTANCE.

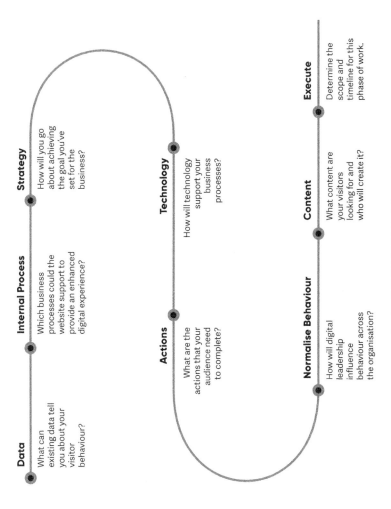

Data

What can existing data tell you about your visitor behaviour?

Internal Process

Which business processes could the website support to provide an enhanced digital experience?

Strategy

How will you go about achieving the goal you've set for the business?

Actions

What are the actions that your audience need to complete?

Technology

How will technology support your business processes?

Normalise Behaviour

How will digital leadership influence behaviour across the organisation?

Content

What content are your visitors looking for and who will create it?

Execute

Determine the scope and timeline for this phase of work.

Go the DISTANCE Model overview

Let's briefly look at each of the eight phases in turn.

Data is everywhere and informs your decision making, providing benchmarks that enable you to measure progress towards your goals. This isn't just technical data such as your website analytics; it should include viewpoints and feedback from internal stakeholders and your customers.

Internal process. Websites are often seen as 'front-facing' marketing-based platforms, but regarding a website purely from a marketing standpoint can overlook opportunities to improve other processes across the business. Exploring process improvement in this way is a key component of digital transformation.

Your **strategy** is a high-level summary of the objective your business wants to achieve. Having defined your strategy, you'll need to explore and map out the tactics you'll implement to deliver it.

Choosing the right **technology** is critically important to the long-term success of your digital activities. Rather than defining them, technology supports your processes and people, and allows you to achieve goals that ultimately enable you to deliver on your strategy.

Audience actions. Build digital products and services with your audience in mind, along with the actions they'll need to take for your respective goals to be met. You want them to be able to achieve their own goals, in turn enabling you to achieve yours.

Normalise internal behaviour. Normalising digital in your organisation is about transforming your organisation's approach to digital. Digital transformation is not about moving from paper to digital or introducing new technology, but redefining your culture to bring together people and technology.

Your **content** answers your customers' questions, sells your products, builds your brand. Without it, you have nothing to show in the digital space. Strong digital performers are publishers, continually creating content around the needs of their customers. Every business now has the capability to be a media company.

Execution. It's easy to be over-ambitious when planning digital projects and campaigns. Your business can't become a digital business overnight, so mapping out a suitable timescale over which you can roll out new features and processes will ensure you have the support of your team and allow you to communicate changes with your customers.

Why *Go the DISTANCE?*

For some companies, despite the huge growth in digital technology and eCommerce, websites are still seen as a check-box exercise. Over recent years, I've seen digital activities become increasingly wasteful, using up both physical and human resources with sometimes scant regard for their value. Content, campaigns and entire websites are created and abandoned, with files merely taking up space on servers across the world after great time and expense has been invested in them.

The word 'distance' is a reminder that you're building and investing in a long-term digital asset. You wouldn't invest tens of thousands of pounds in new plant and equipment only to scrap it two years later, would you? Yet I've seen this happen repeatedly in digital projects. It's too easy to rip up what you have and start over. In this way, digital is one of the world's largest polluters, but so far, it seems to have escaped scrutiny by climate activists. It's vital for everyone's benefit that companies are making sustainable investment decisions around their digital strategies, and the Go the DISTANCE method will bring clarity to that process.

Using this book

The book is split into three sections. Part 1 explains the importance of a clear brief with a realistic budget, as well as highlighting common mistakes business leaders make when planning a new website.

Part 2 walks through the steps of my DISTANCE process. You'll see why each step matters and how they interrelate, as well as where to find the information you need to make informed decisions about your next website project.

Finally, Part 3 explores some of the things business leaders do that fuel their companies' growth, develop their culture and allow them to scale. This section includes a list of recommended resources and tools that I regularly use in my own business to deliver incredible results for my clients.

Companion website

Alongside this book is a companion website, https://gothedistance.website, where you can find additional resources and worksheets to support you as you Go the DISTANCE.

One of the most important things when planning your digital strategy is to know where you're starting from. In fewer than five minutes, calculate your score to benchmark your current digital marketing performance and obtain a free report personalised to your business.

Get your score today by going to https://gothedistance.website/score.

PART ONE
A NEW WEBSITE PROJECT

'The beginning is the most important part
of the work.'
  Plato

1
Why?

'Definiteness of purpose is the starting point
of all achievement.'
—W Clement Stone

Have you decided you need to build a new website?
Perhaps you're at the start of an exciting journey
to launch a product or service, or now is the opportunity you've been waiting for to step up your digital
game. You might be planning a brand-new website, or
have identified enough shortcomings in your current
site that suggest it needs to be completely re-built.

The promise of a new website is an exciting time for
a business. Whatever your motives for starting this
project, there are huge opportunities in front of you.
These could include eCommerce and selling your

products or services online, introducing new efficiencies into the business by connecting to other software, or improving the customer experience so you can build loyalty and enhance your brand. There's a promise of success: better positioning in your marketplace, new leads and sales growth.

But like most things in life, none of this happens by accident. You need a clear plan to deliver these results because there are so many different ways you could go about it. All too often, a new website is cited as the solution to all a business's problems. Fixing your website may well address some of the challenges you face, but if it's to enable your business to work and become a success, you need to think well beyond it.

As websites have matured, they have become able to do lots of different things for your business. In some ways, it's now easier than ever to build a website using 'readymade' platforms such as Wix, Squarespace and Shopify. You can put together a website in an afternoon that enables you to get your message out there, start building an audience and create revenue. At the same time, though, websites (and the behaviour of their audiences) are more complex than ever before, so it's crucial to invest in the right level of functionality that will result in a digital asset allowing you to scale your business.

Too many times, I've seen how the planning and research required for a new website are 'brushed over' in a rush to hide the embarrassing site that has been long overlooked and neglected. 'It would be great if we could get the site live by the end of the month' is a request I've heard on plenty of occasions, and I continue to see ridiculously short deadlines in invitations to tender. Or, I've seen examples where the vision for a new website is so focused on giving the business 'this one thing', everything else the website can offer is cast aside in favour of the perceived silver bullet.

If you view your website as an asset to your business, one that will provide value to your customers by solving their problems while building your brand through nurturing relationships and supporting your growth with a continual flow of sales leads, you can't build it in an afternoon. Nor will it be completed by the end of the month.

If this new website you're building is truly going to make a difference to your organisation, you need to start with a detailed brief that can be challenged through a well-structured planning process. Spending time planning your website to understand how it fits into your wider business, where it can have the greatest impact and how it can support your growth is an investment in itself. In some cases, this process can even save you money by validating your ideas and simplifying the overall requirements.

The key questions to ask yourself are *why* and, more specifically, *why now*?

- Why do you need a new website?

- Why do you need this new feature?

- Why can't you work with your existing website?

- Why would now be a good time to build a new website?

- Why haven't you done this before?

Your 'why' answers will focus your mind on the **problem** you're facing rather than going straight to a perceived solution. At the point you run out of answers, do you feel like you've been able to justify the need and the timing for the project? On what basis did you come up with your answers? Will they add value to your clients and customers?

If you found this exercise relatively easy, then it's likely you already have compelling reasons to build a new website. Writing a brief should be fairly straight-forward, and my eight-stage Go the DISTANCE meth-odology will provide you with a framework and the knowledge to get the best value from it.

Websites are still important

With the growth of social media and other publishing platforms over the last decade, some business leaders have raised the question of whether a website is still relevant. It is true that audiences have become more fragmented, and there are now plenty of third-party sites and marketplaces you can use to promote your business or sell your products.

Publishing content to social media sites or platforms like Medium can be great for reach and engagement. Selling products on Amazon's marketplace may be a quick route to market. Crucially, though, you don't own these platforms. They're not assets in your business. Platforms can change their policies – Medium could remove your content at any time, and a minor breach of Amazon's strict seller policies could see you taken from its marketplace with nothing to show for it. They may even disappear through failure or takeover, which could impact on how your content is found or perceived.

While the likelihood of this happening may be slim, the closure of platforms like Google Plus and Vine, as well as stories of Facebook accounts being blocked or deleted, make it a possibility worth considering. I'm not saying don't use social media or other platforms if they're appropriate channels for your content, but owning a website allows you to build trust in your brand and provides an authoritative source for all things that relate to your company. In addition, if you're going to run any form of lead generation or sales campaign that relies on being found by search engines or ad clicks, the results will almost certainly be dependent on the strength of your website.

Do you really need a redesign?

A website redesign project for a typical product or service business with a yearly turnover above £1m is no small undertaking. Support your decision-making process with data and evidence from a range of sources, pointing to specific reasons why your current website is letting you down and why a redesign is your only option. Committing to a redesign project is expensive and carries risks, so it's not enough for you to look at your current site and say you just don't like it anymore.

One of the basic reasons I created my DISTANCE method was to encourage a more sustainable approach to website ownership. I've seen plenty of instances where company leaders fall into the trap of a redesign cycle, which can become an expensive habit. They get fed up with their current website, so decide to start again with a redesign. The new site looks great for the first six months or so, then the enthusiasm of owning and using it begins to wear off. Content stagnates, people move on to new roles or something changes within the business, but instead of giving the site the same care and attention they did during the build, editors or marketing execs decide to shoehorn content into a page that was designed for a completely different purpose. Pages look broken, links fail as things get moved around, and before long, it all looks a bit of a mess. Eventually, someone will revisit the website and feel such shame and embarrassment, they immediately decide it's broken and needs to be replaced.

If this cycle repeats every two to three years, it will add significant financial expense to your business, and the stop-start nature of this approach is disruptive for both you and your customers. It's also incredibly wasteful as the time and effort people once gave to the site is thrown away with scant regard for any value that could be salvaged.

Don't get me wrong, there are times when a full website redesign will be the only practical option. Websites are a technology product and sit within several constantly evolving environments, so at some point, it's likely that the cost to maintain your site will outweigh the cost of rebuilding it. But, by following the approach outlined in this book, you can break the boom-and-bust cycle of website ownership by investing in a longer-term asset that you can enhance over time, rather than discard every few years.

Redesigns carry risk

Project redesigns aren't a silver bullet to fix a 'broken' website, and done without the proper planning, they can be incredibly wasteful exercises. A new website won't make any difference at all unless the business as a whole embraces a new culture towards it and its surrounding digital ecosystem. These cultural shifts take time and require leadership to put them in place to avoid the same conversations cropping up every few years or each time there's a change in management. There are technical risks, too, with a new website; not least in relation to budget and scope challenges, but also when it comes to benchmarking performance and maintaining search engine visibility.

Perhaps one of the biggest risks with a redesign is planning and migrating content. Simply copying the content from the old site to the new one would be a wasted opportunity and incredibly short-sighted. The quality and structure of the content in your website is one of the primary influencers of its overall performance, from the way people perceive your brand to how their problems are solved and the actions they need to take.

On the flipside, changing all your content and introducing a new site structure requires careful planning to avoid confusing existing users or damaging your search engine rankings.

A redesign is a good opportunity to get rid of the things that you know aren't working, but it's crucial to ensure you take stock of what *is* working and where your visitors find value in your existing site. There's little point in simply throwing everything out the window in a redesign. It's even fair to say a brand-new site won't be 100% perfect when it's launched (is anything ever 'perfect'?) and that's where accepting continual improvement is a given with website ownership, allowing you to refine your website over time.

Digital goes beyond your website

As you're considering either a new website or a redesign, it's important to pause and consider the wider business impact and benefits. It is so much more than 'just a website' and should be having a positive impact on multiple audiences and teams across the business. A new website might look great, but if that's all it's achieved, the true benefits it could bring aren't going to be realised.

Websites are collaborative projects, but while it's great to seek a range of inputs and opinions, clearly not everyone can be involved. Identify key stakeholders and their level of involvement early on in the project to prevent it from being derailed through an overabundance of ideas and opinions.

As you start on your journey to plan a new website, you need to keep in mind that building it isn't about the website itself. Digital is never 'done'. Following the eight-step process outlined in this book will provide you with a framework to build a digital strategy and a high-performing asset that will literally Go the DISTANCE.

Summary

To make sure a new website or a redesign will work for you and your organisation, first of all, you need a plan. And to create your plan, you need to know the reasoning behind your desire for a new website. Is it really necessary? If so, why? And why now?

Even in the modern world of social media and other platforms, a website is still important. After all, you own your website and can use it to show the world how you want your brand to be known. Using my DISTANCE methodology, you can make sure that you avoid the cycle of redesigning your site, loving it for a while, getting bored, stagnating, then starting again. But I'm not saying you build a website, and then just leave it to look after itself. Remember that digital is never done.

Actions

Using the learnings from this chapter, ask yourself the 'why' questions we covered earlier.

Then ask yourself whether your current website has suffered from a lack of investment. If it has, how will you avoid a new site from suffering the same fate? Is a redesign really necessary to solve the problems with your current website?

Ask colleagues for a critique of the website to get a general view of how it works and how it's used. You can also explore feedback from your customers to get their opinion of your website and what they look for in it.

What are the wider benefits that a new website can bring to the business beyond simply 'looking better' than the current one? Finally, for all you hope to see in a new website, is your current website *really* stopping these things from starting today?

2
The Website Brief

'If you define the problem correctly, you almost
have the solution.'
—Steve Jobs

A brief is an essential component of your website
project as it directly impacts on its end result and
future successes. Not only this, it can also determine
whether your website grows to become an asset within the business or an expense that fails to provide a
return on your investment. Your brief is a business
plan for your website that sets the context of why you
need it, the problems it will address within your business and what success would look like in the months
and years to come.

A detailed brief is the most important document in any design project, and as such needs to be one of the earliest documents you prepare as part of your planning process, regardless of whether you will build the website with an internal team, freelancer or external agency.

Why the brief is so important

Let's step away from your website for a moment and consider a new house build. Would you start a project like this without a plan? I suspect you'd approach an architect to discuss your ideas for the house, and maybe consider working with specialist companies to plan the kitchen, interior styling and home entertainment systems.

The conversations you'd have with these individuals would focus on what you want the house to achieve and how it will work for you. You'd be expected to know what style of house you're wanting, how many rooms you need and how each room will be used so the final space is practical and purposeful. The building will need sufficient space for accommodating and entertaining friends and family so you can do the things you enjoy, while allowing for the things that are important to you, such as plenty of light, sustainable materials or a great view.

They'll also ask about your budget, and this isn't a trick question! You could build a house with a £200,000 or a £2m budget, but the approach and outcomes at each level will be different. A smaller budget doesn't necessarily mean you can't have what you want, but it will likely mean you will have to make compromises and maybe some tough choices to ensure each of your requirements is satisfied.

Exactly the same scenario comes into play when you're planning a new website, although building it will be far more accessible to a wider audience because of the availability of low-cost tools, coupled with the fact that no website is permanent. It's easy to hit the 'undo' button in any planning process, which has obvious implications when you're building a house, less so with a website.

Identify the problems that need solving

With technology evolving so rapidly around us, it's easy to recognise the problems it helps us solve and how it brings tangible improvements to our daily lives. As a result, when we're thinking about websites, we can have a tendency to jump to a perceived solution rather than analysing the challenges at the heart of the business.

Our brains are excellent at articulating a desired outcome when we don't understand how something works: we get straight to point of explaining what we'd like to happen or be able to do when the problem is fixed. This is much less clear with websites and apps. It's easy to follow in the steps of others who appear to have already solved the same problem as ours, but everyone has a reason for doing something their way, and I daresay they were in the room when those decisions were made. We weren't.

Be cautious of sharing statements with your management team like 'We need a mobile app' without understanding how an app will actually add value to your audience or business. 'Because this is what Amazon does' may well be the case, but using this as your rationale doesn't revolve around the needs of *your* business or consider the fact that it's not Amazon.

A better problem definition here might be 'Shipping low-value orders is costly, so we need to increase our average spend per customer, and data tells us most of our customers are shopping on a mobile device'. An accurate problem-definition statement such as this can lead to several possible routes to solving it, because there are likely to be a range of approaches that each have their own respective pros and cons.

Working with constraints

Just about anything in digital is possible, but as well as highlighting all the things you want to achieve in your brief, it's also important to balance this against the inevitable constraints. These are barriers such as time and cost that make it hard for you to include everything on your wish list for the site.

Some constraints will be variable and easily overcome, while others will be fixed and beyond your control, but by including them in your brief, you open up the opportunity for creative problem solving and innovation. As your brief is shared among other people, within either the business or a creative agency, everyone's individual perspectives, experiences and skills can find ways to circumvent some of the constraints, or even remove them altogether.

Time, cost and scope

Just about every project ever managed has been defined by three things: time, cost and scope. Each of these factors determines the quality of the final outcome. Not only are time, cost and scope individual constraints, but they're also interdependent on each other. Changes in any one constraint will require an adjustment in the others to compensate or quality will suffer.

Think of these constraints as a camera tripod with three legs. A picture taken on an angle can still capture a moment well, but if all the legs aren't roughly the same length, the composition won't be as effective (or could even miss the intended subject altogether).

If any one of the legs is much longer or shorter than the others, the tripod will fall over.

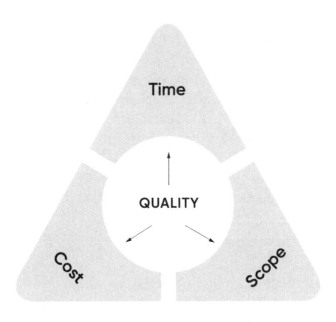

The project management triangle

If the scope of a project is disproportionately high compared to the available time or budget, the quality will suffer. To maintain the scope you desire, increase the budget and time or scale the deliverables back to fit with the timeframe and likely cost. If getting the project out of the door urgently is paramount, then you will almost certainly have to cap the scope with certain deliverables removed or phased in over time if the quality is to be maintained.

It's possible to simplify this model slightly when it comes to planning software or website projects by presenting three requirements, but it's only possible to choose two options:

- Quality

- Speed

- Cheapness

Choosing quality and cheapness will take time to deliver. Opting for quality and speed will force the budget up, while demanding a high standard of quality with fast delivery carries a risk of failure and needs to be avoided.

Other constraints

Time, cost and scope aren't the only constraints that can affect a project. Others might include regulatory procedures and compliance, availability of resources (usually people) or an over-dependency on third parties. There may also be more 'uncomfortable' constraints that don't always present themselves clearly, for example political infighting over how certain features are to be delivered or whether they should even be included. All of these can cause delay and weaken morale across the project team.

As projects become more complicated, it can be worthwhile creating documents like a risk register and a responsibility matrix to identify and mitigate risks. Having a clear plan supports smooth delivery as the project progresses.

Budgeting for your website

Budget is typically the most common constraint for a website project, with costs from different agencies often varying enormously, causing difficulties in making direct comparisons. In 2018, the British Army reportedly spent an eye-watering £113m on a new recruitment website. I can't imagine how costs could get anywhere near this level, but not only that, the website also turned out to be fifty-two months late![1]

The budget requirement for a website is driven by multiple factors, but as a general rule, a larger set of features will require more complex development with a longer timeframe for delivery. In addition, as these features become more complex, so too does the need for experienced developers, greater testing and potentially greater costs to support and maintain the site.

Digital projects will usually be categorised as a marketing expense (although some websites, or even elements of a website, may be classed as IT spend). There are no hard and fast rules about how much to spend on a website, or what a website will cost. Sources online

---

1   BBC News, 'Army's £113m recruitment website "was 52 months late"', BBC, December 2018, www.bbc.co.uk/news/uk-46561779

suggest a marketing budget of anywhere between 7% and 16% of your overall revenue, with suggestions that around half of this should be directed towards digital channels.[2] For a company turning over £1m, this would suggest a total marketing budget of £100,000, with annual digital spend in the region of £50,000.

Even with these benchmarks, investment in websites will vary widely depending on factors such as your routes to market, the competitiveness of the sector you operate in and your ambitions for growth. If you're selling products exclusively through an eCommerce website, then it might be that you spend almost your entire marketing budget on providing your customers with a great experience online. Sectors with a high human touch, on the other hand, may see a much lower digital spend, but one thing is a certainty following the global pandemic: average spend on digital channels is likely to increase across the board.

Now let's talk about each of the considerations to include when planning not only the budget you might need for the website build, but also sufficient 'change' to promote and utilise it once it's in place. Your website has the potential to become one of your highest-performing assets, but it will need regular investment to test and adjust it so its performance is optimised over time.

2   E McIntyre and AM Virzi, 'CMO spend survey 2018-2019', Gartner For Marketers, 2018, https://images.gartnerformarketers.com/Web/ Gartner/%7Bb5a5ad17-bf4c-4ce4-adb3-4eed347852c8%7D_CMO_ Spend_Survey_Note_Repackage_FINAL.pdf

Discovery

Every project will require a briefing and planning stage. For me, this is the most vital part of the project (and the reason for this book). Too often, emphasis is placed on the finish line and getting a new site live, with the result that features are under-used or under-perform, failing to support growth.

The other problem I see in the early stages of a new website project is that when the decision-making process becomes drawn out, some people see this as part of the discovery phase. While they might have had plenty of conversations that culminate in an agreement to work together, these are sales conversations that tend to be shallow in depth until the agreement has been reached.

There are lots of elements that need to be part of the discovery and planning stage and these will be covered in the chapters that follow.

Website build

The build element of the website will almost certainly require the majority of your budget. This includes creative tasks such as wireframing layouts that allow content and functionality to be mapped out on each page and the visual look and feel of the site. This is often called user experience (UX) design, but this too must look beyond your website and consider the overall experience of your customers. This means considering what prompts their need, where their journey starts, which touchpoints should be considered and what their end goals are.

The technical build will follow this, where developers are writing the code to enable the designs to work in a web browser and provide the functionality to make the site work. This stage includes elements like on-page interactivity and connecting to databases or other systems.

Testing and beta launch

Testing a new site is vital to ensure everything works as it should and is as agreed in the project scope. A new site will usually be built on a development server so it can be shared with colleagues or a subset of customers for you to gather feedback.

The more complex the site, the more important the testing phase is to ensure there's no damage to your brand reputation. You don't want to be launching a site that doesn't work properly!

Hosting

Website hosting refers to the server environment used by your website so the world can access it. A more complex site with high traffic or one that provides business-critical services will demand a more robust (and costly) infrastructure to minimise the risk of a single point of failure.

Hosting can be determined by visitor traffic and the level of transactional processing the server will need to do. The location of your audience can also play a role, with global companies potentially having to consider additional elements such as a content delivery network to provide high availability and better performance relative to the location of their visitors.

Servers are responsible for a large part of your site's performance and sit on the frontline when it comes to defending you from cyber-attacks, so a secure and resilient environment is crucial to protect your website. A saying I've always used is 'Cheap hosting is expensive hosting' to emphasise that cutting costs here can be a false economy.

Training

You and your team need to understand how the website works and how you can get the best value and results from it. As the site is being built and prior to handover, ensure everyone knows how it works, from both a customer's perspective and a management point of view. Managing your content, adding products, creating landing pages and building data capture forms are all tasks for your team to be familiar with, where this level of functionality has been built into the site.

Technical support

With the internet having so many moving parts, things can and will go wrong with your website. Technology will let you down at some point and, as luck will have it, it will most likely be at a crucial moment. You need to know who's responsible for each element of your technology 'stack' so you can find resolutions and put fixes in place quickly, minimising the impact on the business.

To this day, it amazes me how many company leaders are unaware of security questions for accounts, or even who their domain name provider is. This is basic information that relates to your business assets, so must be held in a central repository where it can be easily accessed by the relevant people.

Additional development

Even with the most detailed and rigorous planning process, once your website goes live, it's still only a version 1.0. You will need to allow for additional development, either on an ad hoc basis, or as part of a wider plan of continual improvement over time. This could mean small amendments based on analytical data, or significant phases of development work to introduce new features on the site.

Third-party subscriptions

These are the tools and services you might want to use as part of your wider marketing, such as email marketing platforms, support ticket management, live chat or review platforms. These are usually subscription-based services, which on their own are relatively inexpensive, but as you expand the connectedness of your site with different services, your spend in this area can soon add up.

Reporting

If your website is to grow and make an impact, then you'll need to measure and report on certain key performance indicators (KPIs). There are plenty of free analytics tools available to support this, but as you find yourself wanting to understand more about your search engine rankings, sales growth, PR mentions or audience engagement, you'll likely need to look into additional platforms that can present this level of detail to management easily.

Promotion

'Build it and they will come' is one of the biggest myths in the history of web design! Your corner of the internet will feel very quiet unless you promote your website across a number of different channels.

Reserve budget to cover a combination of email campaigns, search engine optimisation (SEO) and paid-ad campaigns among other tactics to ensure you have visibility in your marketplace. Costs can vary widely depending on the competitiveness of your sector, your growth ambitions for the business and the size of your audience.

Software

Depending on the software that underpins your website, you may have licensing fees to consider or plugins that you need to buy to install on your site. There is plenty of excellent open-source software available for free, although a word of warning: 'free' doesn't always mean it's the cheapest! Licensed software may attract annual renewals that allow you to continue to benefit from ongoing updates as they're released, or there may be support programmes offered by vendors or agency partners you're working with.

It's vital to ensure that any software, whether it's free or otherwise, is continually kept up to date. The environment around your website is constantly changing, with new cyber threats uncovered every day. You may not think you're a target because you consider yourself to be too small or you don't collect online payments, but hackers take no prisoners when they find opportunities to use a website for illicit gain. Being the owner of a compromised website carries a far greater likelihood of 'when' rather than 'if', so it's crucial to minimise the risk of your site being the target.

Content creation

Creating content for your website is often hugely underestimated, and can be the straw that breaks the camel's back. Taking aside ongoing blog posts or news articles, a corporate information-based website can quickly escalate to over fifty pages that require content, including written copy, photography, video and, increasingly, audio as well. eCommerce sites will have at least as many pages as there are products to include, and as this space becomes ever more competitive, engaging product pages need to have plenty of information well beyond a simple description.

Remember that the content process doesn't simply stop when it's all prepared. Once you've created your content, it needs to be added to the site. This is rarely a copy-and-paste exercise; to ensure a positive overall experience for visitors, you'll need to identify related content sections in other parts of the site so you can add relevant links, and consider how this content will then be optimised for search engines and overall performance.

Summary

While your brief should be as detailed as possible, think of it as a discussion document to help you formulate your ideas rather than a definitive set of instructions. It will likely evolve over time and take you towards the minimum deliverables that allow your team to estimate timelines and cost indications.

Without a creative brief, a project is quite literally in freefall from the outset. With no definition of the desired outcomes, there will be a lack of direction; timescales without deadlines or milestones; no clear line that indicates when done is done; and nothing to benchmark future performance against.

While a brief may include certain technical elements for your website such as software considerations, or existing tools and platforms already in use in the business, don't be too prescriptive to begin with. Focus on what's important for the business and your audience, and follow the process we're about to get stuck into so the rest falls into place.

Actions

Using the learnings from this chapter, ask yourself:

- Have you framed the problems that the website should solve in a clear way?

- Will you need to make compromises in the time-frame or scope to be able to maintain the quality of work?

- Is your timeframe realistic, given the other tasks that need to be completed as part of the project?

- Do you need to reconsider how your budget will be allocated to help with controlling costs and maintain the quality of work?

- Are you ready to start a new website project? Are there other activities that sit on the critical path that could better prepare you to start a new website? (Although don't use these as excuses *not* to start!)

You can start the process of writing your creative brief by heading across to the resources section on https://gothedistance.website. This will give you a basic structure to gather your ideas and thoughts so you can share them with colleagues or an external developer.

From here, let's begin the process of Going the DISTANCE.

PART TWO
EXPLORING THE DISTANCE

'Sometimes you need to distance yourself
to see things clearly.'
    John Spence

3
Data

'Take nothing on its looks; take everything on
evidence. There's no better rule.'
—Charles Dickens, *Great Expectations*

W e all make assumptions about why something
happens or the steps that might have led to an
event. There's nothing wrong with making assumptions; in fact, they provide us with a start point for
challenging them and unearthing the facts behind them.

With websites and digital platforms collecting vast
amounts of data in the form of analytics and behavioural insights, there's no reason to make investments
in digital on the basis of assumptions alone. I doubt
you would buy a house without having a survey completed, and I'm almost certain you will have been

influenced by an online review prior to buying something or booking a hotel. These are both examples of types of data that influence your decision making to support a positive outcome.

Data is the first step in my DISTANCE method. From the outset of planning a new website, you need to establish the evidence to support the whys you considered in Chapter 1. Data doesn't just apply as you're planning a new website, though; continually refer to data to support the evolution and optimisation of your website over time. Getting into a habit of making evidence-based decisions early in your project will serve you well for the future.

It's impossible to over-state the importance of data as a key input into your business planning and reporting. With vast amounts of data being generated every second, the biggest challenge for most company leaders is turning it into valuable information.

If you look at businesses like Facebook and Amazon, they're first and foremost data businesses, collecting huge amounts of information about an individual's browsing and buying habits, continually testing new approaches (that in most cases are so subtle, you won't even notice them) and optimising their revenue models to enable their continual growth. Amazon founder Jeff Bezos was even quoted as saying, 'We don't make money when we sell things. We make money when we help customers make purchase decisions.' The approach behind Amazon's astronomical growth isn't simply to increase its sales volume, but to use data to positively inform and influence its customers' buying decisions.

While data from websites and marketing platforms is all around us (and don't forget offline data sources), extracting and grouping the relevant information to a specific situation can be overwhelming. Even where quality data exists, many company leaders struggle to identify the actions to take in response to what it tells them. With a common problem being a lack of KPIs or benchmarks against which business outcomes can be measured, we'll spend the rest of this chapter looking at some of the key sources of data to inform decisions for your new website, and what to read from them as you build a case for your project scope.

Types of data

Data takes two forms: *quantitative* information, which is factual numeric data often seen in spreadsheets and reports, and *qualitative* data, which is more subjective because it can include a range of views and opinions from individuals or groups.

Quantitative data is based on measurements of factual information about which there can be little argument. Essentially, it's the 'how much and how many', giving a clear picture of current or historical facts which are then open to interpretation. If 10,000 people visited your website last month, that's a fact that can't be changed.

As you compare results over time and see that visitor numbers are increasing or decreasing, then it's important to understand why this is by looking at *qualitative* data sources. Qualitative data is more subjective. This doesn't make it any less accurate, but it is open to broader interpretation and may require deeper analysis to identify trends.

If you ask ten people how easy a website is to use, you'll get ten different answers. None of these answers will be right or wrong. What qualitative data allows you to understand is the reality of individuals and groups based on their own specific circumstances or life experience. When you analyse this data, a picture will emerge to explain why only 10,000 people (rather than, say, 20,000 the month before) visited your website.

Quantitative data, although widely available, gives insight on the past, but crucially doesn't reflect the human experience of using a website while trying to achieve a particular goal. Qualitative data can be more complex and time consuming to come by, and will usually require a series of interviews, polls or focus groups, but given that websites are used to solve the problems your audiences face, being able to research and gather both types of data is essential to achieving successful results.

As the size of your business and the criticality of your digital platforms grow, data collection and research become more vital to optimise your product or service. High-traffic eCommerce sites like thetrainline. com or Confused.com have invested heavily in their own research teams and are constantly testing and measuring the credibility of their UX. The risk and potential cost from making incorrect assumptions on this scale would simply be too great, so their obsession with customer data has positioned both companies as leaders in their respective sectors.

Let's now look at some of the typical data sources for your website.

Website analytics

It's rare to find an existing website that doesn't collect statistics about its visitors. The popular platform for doing so is Google Analytics, which is used by 84.1% of all websites that use a traffic analysis tool. This equates to 54.6% of all websites.[3] For the vast majority of sites, Google Analytics is entirely free, plus it integrates seamlessly with other Google products,

---

3   W³Techs, 'Usage statistics and market share of Google Analytics for websites', W³Techs Web Technology Surveys, no date, https://w3techs.com/technologies/details/ta-googleanalytics

notably Search Console and Google Ads, so it is by far the most widely supported analytics platform and requires minimal setup to start collecting data.

Although Google Analytics is quick and easy to install, many companies just do that, and then fail to take advantage of some of the advanced (and useful) features it offers. For example, you can add event and campaign tracking to give you greater insight into which links are the most popular and how success-ful your individual campaigns are. If your website uses its own search tool, a little extra configuration will show you not only which search phrases your visitors type into your search box, but whether they actually provide a result which answers their query.

Website analytics will be one of the most valuable sources of data for a new website, telling you how people use the site, the most popular content, and even what level of resources your hosting sever might need to ensure it can cope with fluctuations in visitor traffic.

Google Analytics data is broken down into four key areas which can easily be remembered by using your ABC:

1. **Audience** – who visited your site

2. **Acquisition** – what brought visitors to your site

3. **Behaviour** – what visitors did on your site

4. **Conversion** – visitors who did what you wanted them to do on your site

These terms are used throughout the menus in analytics, making it easy to navigate to the appropriate section to access the data you need. The most valuable metrics for websites are:

- **Source** – where your visitors came from, eg a search engine, direct visit or social media post.

- **Average time on page** – the length of time a visitor spent on each page; in other words, this is a measure of how engaging they found your website content. This is particularly important for your key product or service pages.

- **Bounce rate** – the percentage of single-page sessions in which there was no visitor interaction with the page. You can investigate a particularly high bounce rate for a specific page, or one that changes suddenly, but referring to the bounce rate for your overall site is likely to give a misleading picture. Also, a page with a high bounce rate isn't necessarily a bad thing if it consistently results in a phone call, representing a conversion.

- **Device usage** – every website should work flawlessly on mobile devices these days, but knowing the type of device your visitors favour can inform design and performance decisions so your customers are getting the best possible experience on your site.

- **Behaviour flow** – this highlights the journeys taken by visitors arriving on your site. It can be daunting to begin with, but it allows you to follow the sequence of pages your visitors look at based on criteria such as landing page, how they found your site and the type of device they're using.

- **Landing pages** – what is the page through which visitors entered your site?

- **Site speed** – the time it takes for your site to load. This is not only an important ranking factor in search engines, but also critical to the overall UX, helping you to remain competitive.

- **Goals** – these are specific actions you want your visitors to take on your website, such as submitting an enquiry form or completing a checkout process.

Google Analytics is an advanced tool that collects data from just about every imaginable activity of your website. While not every site will need to take advantage of its full capabilities, get into the habit of referring to this tool regularly if your website is going to sit at the heart of your digital business.

Checking in on your analytics data regularly can help you to identify problems, spot new opportunities and, of course, ensure each campaign you run is getting the results you were hoping for. Having access to this level of data when you're planning a new site is essential, but it doesn't necessarily give you the full picture, as you'll see in the next sections.

Platform analytics

Depending on the channels you're using, you will likely have access to analytics that provide platform-specific data insights. This might be similar data to that found in your website analytics, although it may be presented in more simplistic formats when compared to Google Analytics. Platform analytics aren't just limited to your website (such as your content management or eCommerce system), but can include social media channels, email marketing platforms and customer relationship management (CRM) systems. Each report may use similar terminology, but you'll find there will be specific metrics applicable to each platform that allow you to measure your performance there.

There can sometimes be an overlap between Google Analytics and platform analytics data. For example, the platform analytics in your email management tool will show you how many clicks there were from a particular campaign, which should broadly match up with your acquisition data in Google Analytics. Small discrepancies may appear between different analytics services, which are generally nothing to worry about, but if you spot any larger differences, explore these to see what could be skewing your data.

Experience analytics

The quantitative data from analytics is incredibly helpful as it gives a broad overview of your audience's activity and behaviour from a multitude of different data points. But while it allows you to draw plenty of conclusions from the information it provides, numeric data will only go so far in offering insights into how people spend their time on your website.

Experience analytics takes data a step further and reflects the human experience people have when visiting your site. These tools allow you to watch what your visitors do with their mouse, which page elements they click on and how their eyes are likely scanning the page in front of them. Experience analytics replicates the sometimes awkward experience of watching someone use your website as if you were standing behind them, allowing you to see whether the assumptions you've made are based on fact, and just how user friendly your site is to both new and returning visitors.

By watching the actual experience of those visiting your website, you can see any errors or bottlenecks that might occur, including so-called 'rage-clicks' (a user repeatedly clicking out of frustration). This allows you to observe critical failings at key parts of your customer journey that would be easily overlooked by quantitative analytics.

Sometimes experience analytics can be incredibly cringeworthy to watch, but it's always valuable learning, and especially effective where you expect visitors to your site to follow a specific process. A checkout is a classic example. You've done the hard work of bringing traffic to your site and they're about to buy from you, but if the checkout process isn't intuitive or introduces extra distractions, all that effort is lost in the final straight.

I once worked with a particular website (that my team hadn't built, I should hasten to add) where I was able to observe customers clicking an email sign-up button rather than the 'next' button as part of the checkout due to inaccurate wording and placement. This type of problem can be invisible to you when you know the process, but immediately becomes obvious when you're watching other people use a site without prior experience of it. It was a simple change to move one of the buttons, based on real UX, with the result being less confusion and an increase in checkout conversions. This not only impacted on revenue, but also meant that the budget being spent on ad clicks to drive traffic wasn't being wasted through a breakdown at the end of the customer journey.

Performance data

Website performance generally refers to how fast your site loads for your visitors, although from a management perspective, performance could also be measured by the number of leads or sales generated, or the level of engagement potential customers have with the site. A fast-loading website has been a ranking factor in search engines for several years and impacts on the human experience of using your website that can't be measured just by looking at your most popular pages in Google Analytics.

No one wants to wait for a slow website to load, especially if they're browsing on a mobile device when bandwidth can be at a premium. Studies by Kissmetrics have shown that 40% of people abandon a website that takes more than three seconds to load, and a one second delay in page response can result in a 7% reduction in conversions.[4] Poor website performance clearly has a cost beyond the simply financial, and with loyalty measured by ease of use, performance is a critical factor in every digital experience.

My team and I saw the impact of this first-hand when we upgraded a high-volume eCommerce store. The changes we made were purely technical to the underlying codebase, so from a customer perspective, nothing changed. This meant that any improvement to the

---

4   N Patel, 'How loading time affects your bottom line', neilpatel.com, http://blog.kissmetrics.com/loading-time

conversion rate was entirely the result of the site being more performant.

In the twelve months prior to the upgrade, Google Analytics showed an above industry average sales conversion rate of 3.16%, with a mean page load time of 6.64 seconds (which was comparatively slow at the time).

In the months following the upgrade, Google Analytics showed us the average page load time had reduced to 3.59 seconds (which, being honest, still left plenty of room for improvement), but the conversion rate had reached 4.35% – an increase of 37% – simply by halving the load time of the site. Overall, this represented a 4.8% increase in revenue without the store making any changes to the look and feel of the site. It was clear proof, if it were needed, that poor performance has a cost.

Google Search Console

Another free tool by Google, Search Console, provides insight into some of the ranking factors that can affect your website and addresses any issues that Google considers impact on the site's ability to rank well. Google Analytics doesn't show the search phrases that your visitors type in to find your website, but these can be seen in Search Console, along with the number of clicks and impressions that result.

Search Console is arguably more useful to monitor ongoing activity on your website, but it can be helpful to identify specific problems that may need to be addressed in your new website. It may also draw your attention to other issues inhibiting your website's overall performance that you can factor into your planning for a new site.

Search engine audits

Almost every website needs to build a strong appearance in search engine results pages. Understanding the technical strengths of your website's SEO can influence how search engines view your content and provides valuable insight that may determine the scope of work required to either improve your results or at least maintain your rankings as you launch your new site.

Search engine auditing tools will typically provide insight on a variety of key ranking factors, usually split between on-page and off-page factors. On-page ranking factors are those which you have the greatest control and influence over because they relate to how well your site has been coded and the structure and quality of your content. On the other hand, off-page ranking factors are those that you can still influence, but you'll likely have less control over. These include inbound links from other websites and your domain name reputation – factors that can take time to build and require continual growth and development to influence.

Free search engine auditing tools are widely available and will usually score your site based on you entering your domain name. Most will provide you with a PDF report and a series of action steps you can take to bring about enhanced visibility in search engine results.

Interviews, focus groups, polls and surveys

As well as being unable to capture details of the human experience your visitors have on your website, typical analytics tools also fail to capture information about your visitors' intentions while they're viewing your website. As people browse websites on different devices and in all sorts of different environments and contexts, having a good understanding of their likely intent is helpful when you're planning your website and content. As an example, a high bounce rate recorded in Google Analytics could suggest that visitors haven't engaged with your content and might have left your site. However, if visitors are looking for a contact email address or phone number, it could be indicative that they have been able to find the information they needed – in which case, the page has probably served its purpose.

Understanding features and why they matter to people can be done using quick polls or more detailed surveys. Depending on how much information you require, interviews or even focus groups may be appropriate to determine the most common tasks that people need to be able to complete on your website. This valuable level of detail can include feedback from customers or internal stakeholders (who will often have competing priorities) and will provide you with insight on how to structure your navigation, content and, even, page layouts.

The key to collecting good data from interviews and surveys lies in asking questions that challenge and encourage people to think more deeply about the answers. In her book *Just Enough Research*, Erika Hall explains that hard questions make your job much easier because they leave you with a stronger argument and greater clarity of purpose. She also makes the very valid point that research is no better just because you have more data. Your focus should be on gathering useful insights in order to meet real-world goals.[5]

Summary

Just as you would be likely to browse customer reviews prior to making an online purchase or booking, use data in the form of analytics and behavioural

---

5   E Hall, *Just Enough Research* (A Book Apart, 2019)

insights to save you investing in digital based on assumptions alone. There are many places you can find this data, such as website and platform analytics (for quantitative data), and experience analytics, focus groups and forums for more qualitative date. Make sure you explore and use these resources to their full advantage, though; some company leaders simply install Google Analytics, for example, and then do no more with it.

Quantitative data is factual, indisputable. It gives you an insight into what's happened in the past, but not why. Qualitative data requires human feedback which is generally more complex to gather, but as the purpose of a website is to solve the problems human beings – your audience – face, it's essential. You need to gather both types of data to achieve successful results.

The best thing about many of the resources we have covered in this chapter is not only do they allow you to gather the sets of data you need, they also help you to find benchmarks against which to measure them.

Actions

Using your learnings from this chapter, check your website is capturing analytics data and look up the key metrics I've described. Look at the other tools you're using to support your website and digital marketing. Do they have their own analytics? Are you using these to their maximum ability? What's the story they tell you?

If you don't have experience analytics, try watching a friend or colleague using your website. Do they take the steps you expected them to follow? Alternatively, there is a range of online testing services you can buy to get direct feedback on the experience of using your site.

Check your website performance using Google Page Speed Insights. How well do you score?

Run a free search engine audit of your site. Does the report make recommendations for improvements? What are the quick-wins that could improve your site without you having to completely rebuild it? Visit your website in Google Chrome and use the built-in Lighthouse audit feature to score it. Right click on your page and select the 'inspect element' menu item. Click the 'Audits' menu item and choose 'Generate Report'.

Finally, you can visit the companion website for the book at https://gothedistance.website to find a list of free resources and tools to support your data collection.

4
Internal Process

'Learning new systems and processes is not
mandatory... but neither is staying in business.'
  —Bobby Darnell

Over recent years, the phrase 'digital transformation' has become the buzzword in business for using technology to improve efficiency and save costs. However, digital transformation isn't a single project, but an ongoing journey that evolves over time, exploring opportunities for performance improvements across the entire business.

For digital transformation to be effective, it needs to take into account three things: culture, process and technology. Only when these three things come together will digital become truly embedded within the business and the benefits realised. Each of these elements is covered in my DISTANCE model, and internal process is the first of them.

Websites in digital transformation

Digital transformation is a common topic in business, but it actually began several decades ago as 'computerisation' took hold. In fact, the first known example of digital transformation was seen as far back as 1951 when J Lyons & Co recognised that computers could make business more efficient.[6] Lyons had over 200 tea shops across London and would use a computer called Leo to manage stock, support deliveries and pay staff. Leo ran the world's first routine real-time office application.

But digital transformation didn't truly gather pace until the 1990s when the popularity of the internet ballooned. As soon as websites connected companies to their audiences, new digital processes were needed to support a higher level of customer interaction.

Digital transformation has advanced since then, with major growth areas being artificial intelligence (AI), machine learning (ML), internet of things (IoT) devices and robotics. But while all of these include

6 'Meet LEO, the world's first business computer', Science Museum, 2018, www.sciencemuseum.org.uk/objects-and-stories/meet-leo-worlds-first-business-computer

new and exciting technology, they can't function without a critical human element.

Digital transformation isn't about moving from paper to online; it's fundamentally about people and process. We humans are the drivers behind technological innovations; with the goal to improve our lives and those of future generations, we sit at the heart of process, and process has the greatest impact on us. At the same time, digital transformation can't succeed without cultural change, so although we're the agents for change, we can also be our own nemesis.

There's wide-ranging evidence to suggest that between 70% and 95% of digital/digital transformation projects fail.[7,8] And while building a website is only a component of digital transformation (and may even be a small part depending on the company and website purpose), if the website is seen as nothing more than a marketing tool, the project risks missed opportunities and failing to provide the expected returns on investment.

How do internal processes influence websites?

As soon as a website is published, you're providing your audience with a direct connection to your

---

7   B Tabrizi et al, 'Digital transformation is not about technology', *Harvard Business Review*, 2019, https://hbr.org/2019/03/digital-transformation-is-not-about-technology
8   R Godfrey, *Be The 5: Digital confidence* (Known Publishing, 2020)

company. You're inviting them to engage with you, whether by downloading a free white paper, buying something or completing an enquiry form. You're expecting certain process triggers to come into the business, so how are you going to respond to them?

Your response will be based on your brand promise to customers, established internal behaviours and the resources of your teams. But what if internal behaviour differs to the expectations of your customers? What if this happens at scale or the response needs to involve multiple departments? How will your business cope and what can you learn from the processes that both succeed and fail?

This is why considering your business's internal process as part of your website build is so important. If your audience and stakeholders are going to get maximum value from your website and it will support the business through its wider digital transformation, you have to look beyond its function as purely a marketing tool.

Strong process drives a positive experience

Planning a new website and thinking about how your audiences and stakeholders will use it provides an opportunity for a blank canvas – not only for the visual design, but for how you want aspects of your business to operate and the level of service you want to provide to both internal and external audiences. The goal is to identify how the website can introduce new efficiencies that save time and reduce costs, supporting business growth and scale.

While there are obvious benefits for the business in refining your internal processes, do this well and you'll naturally provide a superior experience for your customers. Most people will probably have experienced the frustration when systems and processes *don't* join up. Healthcare has been an example of this. There are so many different possible touchpoints, with personal records being held in multiple locations and assigned to several health professionals, migrating these to coordinated digital systems and training people to access them has been a gargantuan task for the National Health Service (NHS) in the UK. On the other hand, our feelings towards a company are given a positive boost when the 'system' works: people follow up on our enquiries and provide solutions to our problems.

Most of us use several digital platforms or services every day, be it in a personal context or as part of our work. The result of this is that our experiences become the standard against which we judge others, leaving the weaker ones exposed to negative reaction and poor feedback. As the majority of people have little patience when a digital experience doesn't work for them, our loyalties will soon be placed elsewhere with services that better meet our needs. Those services built around a deep understanding of customers and everything they might need to do without them having to resend an email, wait for approvals or speak to a customer contact centre simply make our lives easier, building loyalty on the back of what most of us now expect as a minimum level of service.

Everyone benefits from better processes

Both internal and external audiences will benefit from strong and refined processes. These audiences include:

- Sales prospects

- Existing customers

- Suppliers and other third parties

- Job searchers

- Employees (especially those working remotely)

- Internal teams such as HR and communications

- Investors

- Compliance bodies such as the Financial Conduct Authority, Solicitors Regulation Authority or the Stock Exchange

Pausing to consider their likely intentions and the tasks these groups might need to complete (we'll talk more about this in a later chapter, 'Actions and

Audience') will help you define how the processes need to work and who to involve in creating them. As a result, people internally can be more confident in their job roles, reducing the time they spend on repetitive administrative tasks, which of course reduces the likelihood of errors and inconsistencies. Including the ability to capture data at each critical step in a process allows you to build up a more comprehensive picture of your customers and their interactions, helping you to further refine the way your processes are structured. Externally, customers can expect higher standards of service (including self-service through the website or other digital channels), and they'll enjoy a more positive visitor experience at whatever stage they interact with you, earning you valuable loyalty as your relationships progress.

Fundamentally, the point is to start the process planning without the influence of technology. Simply introducing technology doesn't provide a fix for poor processes; these have to be built on sound foundations that consider human behaviour at each step, before you apply technology to improve the process or the experience. Once you've established a process, it can always be refined to fit a given technology at a later stage, but design the core elements of the process against non-negotiables such as compliance frameworks or policies, brand values and customer expectations.

Content review process

This may surprise you a little as it's not so much a business process, but more specific to your digital output. Nonetheless, it's particularly important to review content that exists on your website from time to time to ensure it achieves three key things: it's relevant, compelling enough to drive actions, and builds trust among your audience.

We'll talk more about content in a later chapter (the C in the DISTANCE method), but for now, just realise it's an important part of planning how you're going to use your website once it's built. Content can age and date, so regularly review it, removing anything that's no longer relevant following a content audit.

The other important aspect of your content is that your strategy dictates how you reuse it across different channels. Content is expensive to create and produce, so it's vital to know how you can repurpose it for different applications for it to reach the widest possible audience.

Introducing technology and automation

While the ultimate goal of robust processes is to deliver a better experience for customers, suppliers and other stakeholders, you can build value and scale from these processes when they're automated, either in part or in whole. Technology doesn't just support processes, it can stand in and take over the heavy lifting, introducing deeper benefits and the opportunity for the processes to scale independently of your resources to hand.

If you already have several types of technology deployed across the business, it's important to understand how and where each process can be supported by the functionality existing within that software. If you're still relatively early in your digital transformation journey and have the freedom of software choices, then knowing the processes the software needs to achieve gives you a natural framework for evaluating and assessing a suitable fit. With so many business processes likely to be triggered by visitors to your website, integrating technology will be a vital component for a successful site (we'll talk more about technology in the relevant chapter of the book).

Personalising automation

Although there's a growing trend towards automation and there are clear advantages to using it, there is also evidence to show that a human touch across digital experiences still matters to people. A survey by customer data platform Segment found that increasingly, people can see when automation has been used, with 71% of consumers expressing frustration when their experience is impersonal.[9]

Back in 1982, futurist and author John Naisbitt coined the phrase 'High tech, high touch' in his best-selling book *Megatrends*.[10] (This would become a title itself in a later work by Naisbitt published in 1999.)[11] His core argument was that people needed high touch to counter the high tech, and as humans, we're always looking for a connected experience. Despite his work around this subject being first published almost forty years ago, his arguments are still strikingly relevant.

This again supports the notion of putting people before technology when it comes to planning your processes. Research by McKinsey found the most successful sales teams strike a balance between human and digital interaction, achieving five times more revenue, eight times more operating profit and, for public companies, twice the return to shareholders.[12]

While automation drives performance, efficiency and scale, it's not a set-and-forget exercise. Successful

---

9   Segment, 'The 2017 state of personalization report, segment.com, 2018, http://grow.segment.com/Segment-2017-Personalization-Report.pdf
10 J Naisbitt, *Megatrends: Ten new directions transforming our lives* (Grand Central Publishing, 1982)
11 J Naisbitt, *High Tech High Touch: Technology and our search for meaning* (Nicholas Brealey Publishing, 1999)
12 C Angevine, C Lun Plotkin and J Stanley, 'The secret to making it in the digital sales world: The human touch', McKinsey & Company, 2018, www.mckinsey.com/business-functions/marketing-and-sales/our-insights/the-secret-to-making-it-in-the-digital-sales-world

automation needs to display relevance and personality, too, and that's dependent on you holding accurate data and having multiple data collection points throughout your processes and customer touchpoints. These two elements are inextricably linked and together will have a significant impact on your customer experience and digital performance, especially when they're supplemented with timely human interactions.

What might you automate through your website?

There are plenty of internal processes that can be supported by your website. In this section, we'll summarise some of the most common.

Sales and lead generation

The most obvious process your website can support is marketing, sales support and lead generation. Your website has the capability to be your most effective sales assistant, reaching around the world and crossing time zones twenty-four hours a day. Most sales prospects will at some point visit your website, and for many, this will be the start of a relationship with you. Capture data at the start of that relationship and use it to follow and support the customer journey through pre- and post-sales.

Although the focus of this book is on planning your website, it's vital to acknowledge that some elements of your processes will happen away from it. This is especially important with the sales process, which is sometimes known as a sales funnel. The concept of the 'funnel' is still valid in that people can move through each stage of the process towards becoming a customer, but the idea of prospects starting at the top of the funnel and becoming customers at the bottom has been superseded by far more complex journeys.

The traditional purchase funnel

The modern lead-generation process is omnichannel and other processes may need to be triggered from interactions at any of your online properties. Ideally, these triggers will be connected to a CRM platform such as Microsoft Dynamics, Marketo or HubSpot. These systems integrate directly with your website, capturing new enquiries, triggering automated emails (that still need to feel personal), assigning internal tasks to ensure follow-ups are managed in a timely way and tracking future web or social interactions. All this is essential not only to follow leads, but also to learn more about your customers so you can see which content they interact with and find the most value from, allowing you to segment them to provide them with relevant content and measure your overall lead-generation effectiveness.

Onboarding processes

An onboarding process is perfect for automation because your customers are naturally giving you their personal information. You've gained their trust, so now is the moment to capitalise on that, deepening their reason for choosing you over your competitors by giving them a great opening experience.

Acquiring new customers is more expensive than retaining existing ones, so providing a great onboarding experience allows you to set the tone of the level of service they can expect. It's an ideal opportunity to explain your process or what happens next and introduce them to key people who might be looking after them. With over 90% of customers thinking that companies 'could do better' with their onboarding,[13] this is an incredibly easy way for you to set yourself apart from your competitors.

---

13 Wyzowl, 'Customer onboarding statistics 2020', no date, www.wyzowl.com/customer-onboarding-statistics-2020-report

Highly engaged customers have been found to be 90% more likely to buy frequently, spend 60% more per transaction and have three times the annual value compared to other customers.[14] Setting the scene and building engagement in your onboarding process can make a huge difference to your lead pool and customer experience.

Onboarding processes are also found in recruitment too. With an increasing number of people starting new jobs remotely, using automation to welcome new employees can reduce fatigue from online meetings and save time by providing information such as important procedures and expectations in their new role.

eCommerce automation

Automation and strong customer-service processes allow successful eCommerce websites that ship physical products to scale up sales volume. Without effective processes at critical stages of a customer's experience journey (and I deliberately say 'experience' rather than 'buying' because the journey continues post purchase), it will soon become a bottleneck, impacting on speed, cost and customer satisfaction.

---

14   Rosetta Consulting, 'Customer engagement from the consumer's perspective', no date, https://static1.squarespace.com/static/5a7103d96957dafbfdbc2537/t/5cae288d9140b70a01ca16 1c/1554917521632

While it's likely that only the largest businesses can automate the entire process (think Amazon), designing the process to be as smooth as possible is within everyone's reach. This can involve selecting a reliable delivery service, automating label creation and timely email notifications so customers know when they can expect their delivery and easily access invoices. In addition, it's easy to automate follow-up emails to ask for feedback and reviews, and for those who don't complete a purchase on your site first time, an abandoned cart prompt with highly relevant, targeted and timely messaging can recover on average $5.81 per recipient.[15]

Other process automation

Process automation you might want to consider as you're planning your website includes:

- Integration with other software, such as your accounts or inventory platform

- Repetitive administrative tasks

- Recruitment

- Editorial workflow (who publishes what on the website)

- Social media

---

15 Klaviyo, 'Ecommerce industry benchmark report: Abandoned carts', Klaviyo.com, no date, www.klaviyo.com/marketing-resources/abandoned-cart-benchmarks

- IoT devices
- AI and ML

Implementing processes

The list of internal processes you can attach to your website will be a long one once you think about the possibilities. As soon as you start mapping out some initial ideas, more ideas will come to you about when and how to add in other touchpoints for your customers and audiences to interact with you. The possibilities really are endless, but before you get carried away and draw out complex diagrams, I urge you to keep things simple to begin with.

As we have discovered, a digital transformation journey is never done. In fact, some people are even known to take umbrage at the phrase 'digital transformation' as it suggests a start and end point.

When I spoke with digital transformation expert Richard Godfrey on the podcast I host, he argued the word *transformation* can conjure up the idea that there's going to be huge change in the business, similar to a caterpillar becoming a butterfly: an unrecognisable change from one state to another, which people are generally wary of.[16] Digital transformation isn't about

---

16   A Armitage and R Godfrey, 'Digital transformation with Richard Godfrey', The Clientside podcast, 2020, https://adigital.agency/podcast/digital-transformation-with-richard-godfrey

becoming something completely different, but making small incremental changes using technology to help people free up their time to do more valuable tasks. It's also about maximising the impact of the customer journey and creating opportunities for your brand to stand out, and ultimately building a stronger business, better equipped for the age we live in.

Another important point is not to make too many changes all at the same time. This risks introducing too much change into the business and makes it harder to see which processes are performing well, and which might need to be refined. To reduce the risk of failure in digital transformation projects, involve people from across the business in both the planning and review stages of process change to ensure you're achieving the maximum impact.

Larger companies in particular tend to have developed in team silos. As I've witnessed, when a digital process doesn't work for someone, they generally won't report it; they'll simply work within the confines and make do with the current process. Signs of this behaviour can be seen on websites where text overruns on a page, images no longer line up as intended or navigation menus become cluttered and confusing. Customers might experience this when actions are promised but not delivered or finding content on the website is difficult. It's in everyone's interest to work together to identify what each team (or business function in smaller businesses) needs the website to do for them and take it all into account at the outset of the project.

When you're involving other people in the website planning process, make sure they realise they're not necessarily going to get the opportunity to influence the entire website. Those involved should be looking not so much at the visual design of the website, but the functionality it offers and who stands to benefit from this, and remain focused on their particular aspect of the site, resisting the urge to be involved with the functionality required by other departments unless there is significant overlap in the process at the centre of the discussion.

Process can be defined by culture

Exploring internal processes can result in a deep dive into management structure, leadership styles, individual values, belief and behaviour systems, roles and policy. All of these added together influence the culture of an organisation. But while they are important considerations when you're exploring process, you don't necessarily want a new website project alone to redefine each of these points. In fact, you need to consider some of them more broadly as part of your company's overall strategy, which we'll come to in the next chapter.

The reason for the focus on internal process for a new website is to understand how it can improve the roles of people within the business by introducing efficiencies. The goal is to consider the tasks people need to do and free up their time so they can focus on those that will have the greatest impact on the organisation or customers. We'll talk more about audiences and personas who will be using your site in Chapter 7.

Summary

Digital transformation is about people and process, so if your website is nothing more than a marketing tool, the project risks missed opportunities and failing to provide the expected returns on investment. While automation drives performance, efficiency and scale, it's not a set-and-forget exercise; it must have relevance and personality, too, along with multiple data collection points and customer touchpoints.

There are plenty of internal processes that can be supported by your website, such as sales and lead generation, onboarding and eCommerce, but I urge you to keep things simple, at least to begin with. Digital transformation is about making incremental changes using technology to help people free up their time and maximising the impact of the customer journey, creating opportunities for your brand to stand out. Make sure you involve all stakeholders in the planning process to look at the functionality the website will offer and who stands to benefit. The goal is to allow people to focus on the tasks that will have the greatest impact on the organisation or customers.

Actions

Using your learnings from this chapter, ask yourself:

- What are the obvious processes that can be improved in your organisation? Explore existing processes and look at their weaknesses.

- Where do mistakes occur? When does this overflow and impact on the customer experience?

- Are there processes that duplicate your teams' efforts between systems?

- Which processes are the most time consuming or repetitive?

- Which processes could your audience or customers help you with via self-service accounts?

- Do your processes focus on human needs? Don't digitise things for the sake of it or because technology allows you to. Look for the genuine problems people have and consider how they can be solved.

Use sticky notes to map your processes, move ideas around and try different scenarios, challenging existing processes and exploring opportunities to improve. Identify measurement options, eg persistence of bottlenecks, customer complaints or mistakes.

And be sure to engage employees in this journey of discovery – get their input to improve job satisfaction, which will help to spread awareness of new processes and reassert established ones.

5
Strategy

'However beautiful the strategy, you should occasionally look at the results.'
—Sir Winston Churchill

Strategy has been the focus of hundreds of studies over recent decades. Its definition, let alone implementation, still causes confusion, especially among smaller businesses.

In reality, every stage in the DISTANCE method is about your digital strategy. The entire concept of *Holistic Website Planning* is about taking a step back from the broad issue of simply 'needing a website' and putting a plan in place to make it successful.

One of the most common misconceptions with websites is that they're completed when they launch. The reality is that the work to make a website successful can only begin once the site is live. Planning a digital strategy can have so many component parts; breaking it down into key stages helps to give focus to specific activities that layer up your approach, so nothing is overlooked and the goals you pursue are realistic and achievable.

In time, as your digital maturity develops, having a specific 'digital' strategy will be of less value and may even seem crazy! Digital becomes part and parcel of everything you do, woven into your entire organisation, forming part of your overall goals and underlying culture rather than being seen as separate or belonging to a different department.

There are plenty of definitions for 'strategy' and it would be easy to accept most of them as being true. The *Oxford English Dictionary* states it is 'a plan of action designed to achieve a long-term or overall aim',[17] but even this simple definition of strategy has a problem.

Digital strategies need to be agile and reactive, so the notion of 'long-term' can be misleading. There's also a perception that your 'overall aim' (typically your vision) has to be something unique and

---

17 Definition of 'strategy', *Oxford Dictionary of English*, third edition, (Oxford University Press, 2010)

groundbreaking, but complicating your strategy unnecessarily risks overwhelming your team members with the feeling that they need to take massive action to deliver it. Depending on what your company means by 'long-term', by the time they eventually deliver the overall aim, the relevance of the achievement may be questionable.

It's unlikely your business is truly unique; there will almost certainly be other companies out there doing similar things, so having both a vision and a strategy as your North Star is important. When you pare it back, though, all your strategy needs to be is a simple plan to ensure you do what you do better than you've done it before and better than your competitors; it isn't necessarily unique. Complicated strategies aren't easily remembered, either, which makes them hard to execute.

Former IBM CEO Louis V Gerstner Jnr was widely credited with turning the fortunes of the company around in the late 1990s. When he joined in 1993, he told journalists the last thing the company needed was another vision; IBM had no shortage of intelligent people with great ideas, but the problem at the time was putting these into action.

In his memoirs, he explained, '... execution is really the critical part of a successful strategy. Getting it done, getting it done right, getting it done better than the next person is far more important than dreaming up new visions of the future'.[18]

Know your starting point

Strategy is about direction and the actions you're going to execute to take you towards your vision. As is the case with any journey, you can't set off without knowing where you're starting from. Not only does this allow you to understand the scale of the challenge you face so you can set realistic objectives, crucially, it also allows you to measure your progress so you can look back on your achievements and lessons learned along the way.

I'd encourage you to measure your own level of digital maturity and strategic activity by visiting the online scorecard at https://gothedistance.website. The questions are designed to offer you a realistic view of your current activities so you can quickly spot areas of weakness and prioritise them for improvement.

When you know your starting point, a good next step is a simple strengths, weaknesses, opportunities and threats (SWOT) analysis. In addition to the results from the scorecard, you need to gain a feeling for what you do well within the business and the areas that you need to improve on. When you're thinking

---

18 LV Gerstner Jnr, *Who Says Elephants Can't Dance?: Leading a great enterprise through dramatic change* (HarperCollins, 2009)

externally, what are the opportunities and threats that your business is facing? What are the things you can and should do to grow, and what are the things that could cause you problems? What's happening in your marketplace? Is there a shift online being led by one of your competitors, or is your market facing particular challenges that in themselves can open up opportunities?

With a view of your strengths and weaknesses, opportunities and threats, it's time to focus on setting goals and how these translate into tactics that will fulfil your strategy and overall objectives.

Goals, objectives, strategy and tactics

It's easy to overthink strategy, so it's worth repeating that it is merely a simple plan to guide you towards your goal(s). In fact, some people may argue that the process you go through to create the strategy is more important than the strategy itself. But let's pause briefly to break down the broader notion of strategy, because although in its simple form it's a plan to get from A to B, there's no one single element to delivering on it.

New York Times best-selling author on strategy Rich Horwath identified that at the heart of most strategy challenges is a lack of clarity over what strategy is and how it differs from other key business planning terms.[19] He established a simple framework called GOST which separates out four words that are often used interchangeably, adding to the confusion with planning and implementing strategy.

His framework defines:

- **Goals** as the broad primary outcome, or vision
- **Objectives** as a *specific* description of what you want to achieve
- **Strategy** as *how* you'll achieve your objectives
- **Tactics** refer specifically to *how* you'll achieve your strategy

The diagram below shows how each element is not only relevant, but also a fundamental component of strategy.

If you think of how a digital strategy might fit into the above model, it could look something like this:

1. Your **goal** or **vision** might be to become the foremost provider of products and services in your industry. This isn't necessarily a website- or digital-related goal, but could be the wider vision held by your company.

---

19 R Horwath, *Elevate: The three disciplines of advanced strategic thinking* (Wiley, 2014)

2. The specific **objective** is to achieve sales of £10m within the next three years, for which 60% of leads will be generated from digital channels. Objectives will generally follow the well-established specific, measurable, achievable, realistic and time-bound (SMART) format.

3. The **strategy** is to communicate the sustainable element of your products and services to prospects who have placed the values of sustainability and ethics in their own strategies.

4. Your **tactics** will be wide ranging, including granular activities such as optimising conversions on your website, encouraging key people to grow their LinkedIn connections and creating campaigns focused on sustainability to reach a specific audience, such as buyers or procurement professionals.

As you can see, goals cascade and proliferate from the top to the bottom, becoming more detailed as you dig deeper into the 'how'. You might find you have three or four primary objectives that support achieving your goal. Below that, there could be several strategies that you follow to achieve the objectives, with multiple tactics that combine to fulfil all the strategies.

At the end of the chain, although not included in Horwath's model, are tasks. These are how tactics are implemented and might relate to the specific skills that you need to work your way back up the chain, achieving each layer.

An overview of the GOST framework[20]

One of the most common mistakes I see when company leaders think they're defining their digital strategy is they start at the tactical level, often by deciding on the tools they will use. They might state that they need to run an ad campaign on Facebook or select a specific CRM because it has been recommended or 'seems popular'.

This puts the cart before the horse, which is easily done because these tools are tangible and widely

---

20   R Horwath, *Elevate*

available, often at low cost to boot. But defining tactics first can let the tool dictate the outcome; it becomes difficult to move away from the perceived solution to the problem you're facing, locking you into a single approach. It must be the desired business outcome that determines the approach (the why before the how), allowing you to identify the most suitable tools and tactics that will enable you to deliver the strategy and achieve your goals.

With clearly defined goals, the way your strategy breaks down will end up looking something like the diagram below.

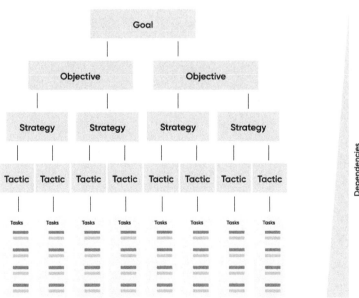

Strategy breakdown based on the GOST Model

For planning your website, the overriding goal and measurable objectives are essential to give context and purpose to what you're wanting to achieve. These inform your strategy, but the level of detail here is still too broad. Although this chapter refers to strategy, the real strategic focus for your website actually needs to be on the tactics that are defined by your strategy. There's little point in having a fancy strategy presentation deck gathering dust on a server somewhere if it doesn't (or can't) translate into the granular and active level of tactical implementation.

Revered Chinese military strategist Sun Tzu has been widely credited with writing, 'Strategy without tactics is the slowest route to victory. Tactics without strategy is the noise before defeat.' The effectiveness of execution in your strategy starts at the bottom with tactics. Tactics break your strategy into small, achievable tasks that individuals can easily add to their to-do list and identify when they've been completed. The short-term nature of tactics gives team members a greater sense of their role in delivering the strategy, and they can enjoy the responsibility and sense of achievement that comes with it.

We'll cover some of the more common tactics in this chapter, but exactly which tactics are most suitable for your particular business or market will inevitably vary. Some of the tactics you decide on will be influenced by other sections of this book, notably 'Data', covered in Chapter 3, and 'Actions and Audience', which we'll cover in Chapter 7.

Choosing tactics

There is an almost unlimited number of tactics you can pursue to support your digital marketing and deliver results as you progress towards your wider strategy. Although there isn't the space to include them all in this book, we can explore the most common tactics and why these are important to consider as you plan your website. You might already be using some of these tactics, in which case, consider a website performance audit to assess the impact they're making on your current goals.

Knowing which tactics you're planning to use prior to starting your website is vital so you can factor in any implications during the design and build phase. In the same way that an architect wants to know how a building will be used and what will be important to the users before they start on their design, you need to decide on the features you'll include from the outset as part of the original website build, as these tend to perform much better than those added as an afterthought. This also reduces the risk of project costs spiralling out of control, timescales being delayed and the ultimate disappointment of discovering the end product isn't sufficiently fit for purpose.

This section is broken down into three key areas, the ABC of digital strategy. Incidentally, I've purposely chosen three of the four areas by which visitor data is structured in Google Analytics. Not only are these areas helpful for breaking down elements of your tactics and strategy, but referring to data on an ongoing basis should be one of your most important tactics in itself. It's key to reacting to an ever-changing environment.

As you consider the three areas, each tactic persists into the next one, but we'll begin by looking at them in different dimensions, allowing you to create a detailed understanding of their appropriateness and relevance to what you're wanting to achieve.

Acquisition

These tactics are all about generating interest and driving traffic. They're not necessarily exclusive to your website, but all have the intention of capturing interest from your audience and leading them towards an action.

Acquisition tactics might include a combination of:

- Search engine marketing (both paid and organic)
- Social media (again, paid and organic)
- Email marketing
- Podcasts

- Video

- On and offline PR

- Referrals, partnerships and affiliates

These tactics don't all have to be deployed together or at the same time. You'll likely have a hunch for which platforms will work best for you, but this is where experimenting comes into play so you can find your niche and place a greater emphasis on the tactics that deliver the best results. Knowing which channels you're going to use to acquire visitor traffic, and how, will allow you to:

- **Plan marketing budgets** for specific channels (paid search, for example) that demand budgets for both running and managing campaigns.

- **Plan content** that adds value to your audience while supporting search engine rankings and getting attention on social media.

- **Allocate resource** to managing each channel and measuring its performance, be that in-house or through an external agency.

- **Select tools and platforms** that will support your tactics such as automating workflow, providing data insights and allowing you to measure performance. These might carry a monthly subscription or require specific training to get the most from them.

- **Plan processes** that support customer growth or campaigns. This might include automation or software integration.

Behaviour

You've done the hard work: you've captured the interest of your audience and they're engaging with you through one of your chosen channels. But what was it specifically that drew them into your brand? And more importantly, what are you going to do now you have their attention?

Tactics at this stage might include:

- Capturing visitors 'in the moment' through live chat or popups

- Adding data into your mailing list and enhancing the experience with marketing automation

- Encouraging feedback through social proof and reviews, on either your website or social channels

- Remarketing to your audience on social media channels or through display ads, encouraging them to return to your brand

- Refining your content focus based on popularity, link clicks and social sharing

- Enhancing the UX on your website with micro-interactions that make your site more memorable

- Developing online communities that identify brand ambassadors

- Adjusting content and acquisition tactics based on behaviours these visitors exhibit

These tactics can allow you to:

- **Grow your audience** and build a list of potential customers for the future.

- **Nurture relationships** by building loyalty over time through adding value without the expectation of it being returned.

- **Provide immediate customer support** through a combination of live chat, video and automated marketing. This will set expectations with your audience by providing customer service twenty-four hours a day as well as allowing you to scale your business.

- **Recapture website visitors** who left your website or failed to complete an action so you can have a second bite at the cherry.

- **Build loyalty** through customers sharing their positive experience of using your website, products or services.

Conversions

Conversions occur when a visitor or a prospect becomes a customer. In other words, they've achieved their own objective that takes you towards yours. A conversion doesn't necessarily relate to a purchase or carry a direct monetary value. A visitor joining your mailing list might not become a customer for several months, but over time, you should be able to estimate the lifetime value a subscriber is likely to provide.

Conversions can include:

- A product or service sold online
- A visitor subscribing to your mailing list
- A lead capture form being submitted from a case-study page
- A form submitted to request a quote or book an appointment
- A link click or a series of page views
- A visitor being able to solve a problem relating to a customer-service type request

It's because conversions usually have a value attributed to them that they're most closely associated with goals and objectives. They're the outcomes that result from the tactics and strategy you pursue. The more conversions you achieve, the closer you get to the desired business outcomes, proving your strategy is working.

Despite conversions being related to outcomes, there are still plenty of tactics that you can explore to optimise your strategy; your job's not done yet! Tactics to optimise conversions include:

- Usability testing
- Page speed analysis
- Other testing and experiments (such as A/B or multi-variate testing)
- Personalisation
- AI and ML

This level of optimisation will allow you to:

- **Provide the best possible experience** to your customers at every stage of their interactions with you
- **Maximise conversions** through identifying problems or bottlenecks at key stages of a defined process, such as a checkout or registration process
- **Make incremental marginal gains** that, when combined, have a significant impact on your goal progress
- **Create personal relationships** that focus on individual customers, providing them with targeted and specific information
- **Operate at the highest level of efficiency** with systems that learn and adapt in real time

Using the ABC of digital strategy

As we've seen, the ABC of digital strategy breaks down into the tactical actions you can take to acquire visitors, influence behaviour and maximise conversions. In my experience, the ABC represents much more than tactics, though. It also represents the level of digital maturity and ambition within a business, and can be thought of as the beginner, intermediate and advanced levels of digital marketing. It reflects the effort and skills to operate effectively at each level, with the knowledge required deepening as you advance from acquisition to conversion.

Those operating purely at the acquisition level are unlikely to have a well-defined strategy. If they do have goals they're pursuing, they're likely to be what's referred to as 'vanity metrics'. These include things like visitor numbers and search engine rankings that might look good on paper, but on their own won't edge you towards your business goals.

At this level, decision making isn't driven by data and activities will often be reactive and made in the spur of the moment. Evidence from SmartInsights suggests that around 45% of companies are 'doing' digital without having a digital marketing plan.[21] That's almost

---

21 D Chaffey, '10 reasons you need a digital marketing strategy in 2021', *Smart Insights*, 2021, www.smartinsights.com/digital-marketing-strategy/digital-strategy-development/10-reasons-for-digital-marketing-strategy

every other company working at this level without a strategy to guide the teams' thinking or actions.

Company leaders who invest time in analysing behaviours on their website and other channels will immediately rise above the majority. They're likely to be looking for opportunities to improve (although they may not spot all of them), listening to their audience and reacting to the information they see in their data and customer feedback. They're probably providing an elevated visitor experience, but there will still be opportunities to optimise this further to maximise conversions.

Those company leaders with tactics at every level of the acquisition, behaviour and conversion stages are likely to have a strong digital-first culture with a well-defined strategy. It's at this level where digital strategies succeed. The actions are regular, process driven and well defined, seeking to prove or disprove hypotheses. Everything is measured, and a few percentage points improved here and there will result in notable progress towards goals, delivering profit, scale and growth.

Measuring progress

With the ABC of digital strategy and one eye on your measurable objectives, you'll be able to establish KPIs that determine whether you're on or off track. These will vary by business type and the goals you have, but in any case, data should be at the heart of your decision making, ensuring it's quick and easy to determine what needs to change if results aren't going the right way. Technology and people's behaviour change quickly and continually need to influence your approach. Getting accustomed to making regular directional corrections is par for the course with digital.

Not all of the tactics I've talked about will work for your site. In fact, sometimes you need to be cautious you don't end up putting your visitors off by having an overly salesy or 'noisy' approach that ultimately detracts from the brand experience they might expect. For some sites, exit intent popups and flash banners offering discounts can be effective, but consider whether these 'smash and grab' approaches fit with your brand, or whether they're potentially a costly price to pay for short-term success, over a long-term investment in building relationships with your audience.

Similarly, there can sometimes be a critical path to follow when you're planning your tactics to ensure you have the right foundations in place. For example, there's little point in committing to a paid search campaign if your content or website landing pages are inadequate. The cost of advertising will end up high and your conversions will be low, with mediocre results at best. A conversion rate optimisation activity is pointless without a minimum threshold of traffic to test against. Adding a newsletter sign-up form won't achieve anything unless there's a compelling reason for prospects to give you their email address.

Take the time to plan each aspect of a campaign which might involve multiple tactics. This is often over-looked, especially when the end goal isn't clear and people rush towards a perceived solution rather than the problem at hand.

Planning budgets

A distinct advantage with your digital strategy is that individual elements of it rarely demand significant up-front financial commitments. Your website will be one of your larger investments as much of your digital activity will be attached to it, but most of the digital products and services to support your strategy can be used on a pay-as-you-go model. In addition, there are several marketing techniques that allow you to collect signals from a subset of your audience before you make large-scale commitments to build new products and platforms.

While a budget will, of course, be needed to push forward with your strategy, there will be plenty of freedom for testing, measuring and reallocating budget as data indicates where it delivers the strongest results. Conversely, though, without a plan in place, there will be enormous scope for wastage with your digital marketing. Focusing on the wrong audiences, failing to analyse results and using paid services without measuring their performance can become a black hole. Ironically, despite this, many companies carry on without a proper plan regardless because they know digital is important, taking the view it's better to be doing something than nothing.

Documenting your strategy

A documented and well-communicated digital strategy will allow you not only to create and build competitive advantage, but to enable innovation and introduce capabilities across the business. Developing new platforms for products and services as well as new communication channels with your prospects and customers can all fall within your digital strategy.

And just because we're talking about a 'digital' strategy, that doesn't mean it's all about technology; a successful digital strategy takes into account the connections between people and how they behave, the systems they use and the priorities they face. In fact, people will be a recurring theme in your digital strategy (and throughout this book) because the availability of technology, tools and data has such a profound impact on the way we all work and behave.

With such a movable feast, being able to adapt and react to external change is crucial if your company's approach to digital is going to deliver rewards. And for that to happen, you need people from across the business to buy in to and support digital's adoption. Involving people in its creation and giving them ownership to deliver certain elements of the strategy will help with this and you'll get broader feedback as your plan takes shape. This approach also helps you to manage resistance to the inevitable change your digital strategy will introduce if it's to be a success and ensures everyone is aware of what it includes, how it will be achieved and what their role will be in delivering it.

Creating a digital culture

The key point with digital strategy is that it's neither a one-off activity, nor will it work in isolation. Strategy provides a focus for decision making and action, but it can be culture that ultimately supports digital's delivery and achievement. We'll talk more about building a digital culture and the impact it can have on your strategy in Chapter 8.

Those working in digital are on a never-ending learning curve and have to be constantly prepared to launch new products, services and campaigns, gauging reaction based on feedback and data before repeating the process. And yes, this will mean things don't always get the desired result first time, but that's OK; so long as you take the appropriate learnings and evolve them into whatever comes next.

Digital campaigns are often seen as a reactive 'tap' that can be turned on in times of need. Actually, this is true, but it comes at a high cost. Digital marketing is a marathon, not a sprint, with success coming from several elements of a strategy all working together. Even if you've identified your audience and know what they're searching for, it takes time to be noticed and win their trust. A single ad campaign might capture their attention, but it's consistency that generates interest and ultimately drives action.

Summary

A successful strategy advances your business's value proposition and builds competitive advantage, but it is dependent on three things. First of all, planning your strategy gives you a framework on which to determine the most appropriate tactics to implement to start your journey. But this is a journey without a fixed destination, travelling roads with plenty of junctions and distractions. Establish your start point and determine what your priorities are, ensuring you have strong foundations in place before attempting to advance your activities without sufficient justification.

As you progress, you need to manage performance against KPIs, feedback and data insights. This will allow you to see how you're progressing and what course corrections might be needed along the way.

Finally, optimising your campaigns will allow you to go the extra mile, maximising the success of your digital assets by delivering tactical improvements that will directly impact the measurable elements of your objectives.

Actions

Using the learnings from this chapter, ask yourself these questions:

- Identify your competitors – what are they doing in your space? How can you differentiate yourself from what they offer?

- How is your current marketing positioning reflected in the goals you've set? What needs to change for you to achieve your goals and create a strategy?

- Complete the online scorecard at https://gothedistance.website. Is the result as you expected?

- Who will lead and take ownership of your digital strategy? Who does it need to be communicated to? What is the timeline you will work towards for delivering the strategy?

- What other resources might be needed for the strategy to be achievable?

- What tactics are you pursuing now? Are they achieving the results you'd hoped for? Are they taking you towards your overall goal? Do they need to change?

- How will you measure progress over the coming months? What data will you use to inform your decision making and shape your boundaries that could suggest you might need to course correct?

6
Technology

'Technology is best when it brings people together.'
—Matt Mullenweg, WordPress Founder

Websites are inherently technology-based projects. The way they're built, the way they're used and how they're measured all involve technology. Where the website will support improvements in internal processes in the business to deliver greater efficiency, you will almost certainly need to have some form of integration with other systems or services.

Being able to identify the software tools currently in use in the business and how they fit together is an essential step to ensuring you're utilising technology in a supportive and productive way. Knowing the shortcomings of your technology 'stack', the frustrations people are having with it and how you want to improve technology in your business is essential to plan and forecast before you make a commitment to a particular platform or service for your website.

Making the wrong technology choices at this stage can seriously impact on the ability of your site to Go the DISTANCE. These poor choices make it more likely that technology will let you down through its failure to work effectively, running the risk of costs escalating out of control as the scope of connecting different systems together becomes more complex.

Even in a relatively simple website, you have technology decisions to make. Just about every website these days is built on a 'platform', which can be fully hosted software, a customised and standalone content management system (CMS) or a tailored code framework. These can all take different forms with their own respective pros and cons that we'll cover later in the chapter. Some platforms allow you to get up and running quickly, but may equally introduce limitations early on to what you can achieve with them. On the flipside, bespoke development takes time and is expensive, so finding a compromise is usually the best option.

Your technology stack

This is all the digital platforms, applications and services you use to run your business. It doesn't just focus on your website or email marketing platform, but the software used across any parts of the business your new website is likely to impact on.

The relevant considerations will naturally depend on the focus and audiences of the new website, but software that you may need to connect to the website could include:

- Accounting software

- Customer support

- CRM

- Email marketing

- Data capture

- Payment providers

- Stock control and inventory

- Job applicant tracking

- Fulfilment and logistics

- Productivity software (such as Microsoft Office or Google Workspace)

- Email services

With the growth of software as a service (SaaS) over recent years, many company leaders will find most of these are provided through cloud-based platforms. In other words, they're hosted on the internet, accessible from anywhere, and will easily talk to other cloud-based services through an application programming interface (API).

Some of the above software may also run 'on premises', which means it's installed somewhere within the business. Communicating with on-premises software can be challenging because there might be internal firewalls to pass through or the software itself may not be designed to integrate with other cloud solutions.

You'll often find different software features overlap with those in other platforms, or can even be combined into a single system. For example, a CRM like Microsoft Dynamics or ActiveCampaign can handle both data capture and email newsletter campaigns along with features such as sales automation and reporting. In fact, there are plenty of apps that might do one thing well, but actually offer several features that overlap with other software you're using. Be careful about adopting multiple systems and not getting the full value from them, or having several platforms that cause confusion over which is responsible for what.

As you've been following my DISTANCE process so far, you'll have already considered the internal processes your website will support, so you're likely to have a feel for the relevant technology it needs to be able to connect with to achieve the outcomes you've identified. You now need to be confident that your website technology choices will give you the freedom to integrate with other software and understand how to use the improved technology and connectivity to grow your business.

A word of warning with implementing technology: like most things in digital, your task doesn't stop once it's deployed. Choose technology based on the goals it's going to help you achieve so you can drive results from within your business, ensuring that your software choices will grow with your business, offering at least the same benefits to a larger enterprise as it offers you now.

Choosing your website technology

There are literally hundreds of different platforms and frameworks for building a website, but making the right choice is vital to avoid finding yourself constrained by technology that should be there to help you. The 'best' platform comes back down to your brief and what you need the underlying technology to achieve for you. An accurate problem statement allows you to base technology on the problems you face and the outcomes you need.

There are typically three approaches to building your website.

Bespoke solution

Bespoke solutions are completely tailored around specific requirements. These typically take longer to develop and come at a greater cost than other options, but the clear benefit is that you will get a platform that does exactly what you need it to. This means it can align closely to your digital strategy, but if that strategy should change, the cost of changing the platform can be expensive. Completely bespoke software can also lead to your strategy being held back by limitations if it doesn't offer you further options for customisation.

Bespoke development will often be the way to go when you have a specific process or functionality that is too complicated or niche to be found in off-the-shelf software. For the vast majority of websites, a fully bespoke build would be unnecessary, but this is dependent on your goals and long-term strategy.

Off-the-shelf solutions

At the opposite end of the spectrum sit off-the-shelf solutions. These are fully featured turnkey platforms that usually include hosting, a selection of readymade templates and hassle-free setup all for a relatively low monthly fee. Websites on these platforms can be implemented much more quickly and cheaply than a bespoke solution, but they often result in compromise with a need to work and grow within more limited confines.

Hosted platforms, including services such as Wix, Squarespace, WordPress.com or Shopify, are typically targeted at smaller businesses and start-ups. That said, these platforms are increasingly providing 'enterprise' services through premium subscriptions for larger companies wishing to scale beyond their lower-level product options.

In my view, these platforms are ideal for dedicated blogs (such as the Co-Op Digital team at https://digitalblog.coop.co.uk), non-core aspects of the business that might have limited reach or new product development that allows companies to test or reach their market quickly and at low cost. They can also work well for building campaign-led microsites that might only have a limited lifespan as there is often a high level of interconnectivity with a wide range of marketing-related SaaS platforms for data capture.

Hosted platforms are generally less effective for larger sites that require features like customer accounts, advanced search functionality or tailored workflow and publishing options. While there can be some room for flexibility, these platforms are designed to be a 'one size fits all' with limited capacity for scale or high traffic. Where this option is available through a fully managed service provided by the platform, it tends to come at quite a high price for most businesses.

Customised off-the-shelf platforms

Most corporate-style websites are built using a combined development approach that offers the best of both worlds. CMSs and eCommerce platforms fall into this category, where they form the scaffolding for a site that can then be extensively customised and developed as necessary to meet the requirements of the brief.

This approach generally offers the best balance of flexibility against development scope and cost, with responsibilities usually split between the vendor and an implementer such as an agency or in-house team. Vendors will oversee the development of the core codebase and ensure its continued security, while an implementer uses the framework it provides to create the look and feel and functionality required.

These systems make use of integrations with other SaaS in the form of plugins. Plugins allow the functionality of a site to be extended, connecting to other systems and services in a way that shouldn't interfere with or compromise the core code.

Popular examples of off-the-shelf platforms that offer extensive customisation options include WordPress, Drupal, Sitecore, Umbraco, Craft CMS and Magento for eCommerce.

With such a wide range of excellent off-the-shelf website platforms available, few websites need to be built on a proprietary system locking you into a single supplier. This may not always be the case for business software, which can have more specific requirements, but generally, an off-the-shelf website platform gives you plenty of options to approach the build, customise the site and integrate with other software for typically a much lower cost than commissioning your own bespoke platform. In addition, the risk is significantly lower, maintenance is less of an issue and you reduce your dependency on a single supplier.

Considerations for your website platform

When you're considering the technology for your website, in addition to exploring how it will work alongside other software you're using in the business, it's important to think about the factors we'll cover in this section.

Total cost of ownership (TCO)

TCO is typically the cost of implementing and maintaining an asset over the course of its useful life. For most websites, the TCO will be based on:

- Availability of design and development expertise

- Software licensing costs

- The cost of third-party plugins or integrations with external services

- Migration costs

- Server hardware and software

- Security and maintenance

- Backup and recovery

- User training

- Testing

Company leaders are naturally looking to invest in assets that carry a low cost of ownership, but cost should never be the sole determinant of whether a particular investment is the most suitable. Take a balanced view on how the technology will support your growth ambitions against risk and cost factors.

Extending functionality and integrations

Some software integrations can be as simple as dropping a few lines of pre-generated code provided from one system into another. Other integrations may be possible simply by installing a plugin that already exists, while more complex integrations will need their own detailed planning and custom development to build.

Many platforms have mature plugin markets or app exchanges which can often reduce cost and time to market, but you need to be cautious about an over-reliance on third-party plugins. The quality of code in plugins can vary wildly (especially the free ones) and some have been known to introduce hidden vulnerabilities to websites. Plugins are often built by individual developers and will fall outside the support scope provided by the platform vendor, so do be on your guard for plugins getting left behind or becoming abandoned by the vendor, especially if they form business-critical functions.

Support

Depending on the complexity of your technology or the business criticality, you will likely require some degree of ongoing support for your website. While this may fall to some extent to your in-house team of developers or an external agency, you may want the reassurance of vendor support. Vendors are responsible for fixing bugs in their software and issuing maintenance and feature releases that enhance and secure the product over time.

Some vendors will release software updates free of charge, while others may charge an annual licence fee. For example, WordPress, a CMS many people will know, is free, but a subscription to its VIP support programme costs from $1,700 monthly. As I've said before, 'free' doesn't always mean free, and 'cheap' carries the risk of turning out to be expensive.

It's vital to assess the business needs for support in the event of a technology failure (which is more likely to be a question of 'when' rather than 'if'). You need to be clear on who's responsible for what under different circumstances.

Security

When you're choosing any technology platform, the ability to ensure it's maintained with patches and security updates is vital.

We tend to hear of cyber-attacks that affect large-scale corporates in the media because these are likely to have the greatest impact on customers. As more data and services move to the cloud, the need for security will only become greater, as will the threats posed by increasingly sophisticated networks of hackers and scammers. In recent years, Sony, Disney, Uber, Yahoo and TalkTalk have all been well-known brands to fall victim to serious data breaches, and the penalties for failing to safeguard your customers' personal data are now significant.

A data breach affecting over 400,000 British Airways customers in 2018 resulted in a record fine of £20m in October 2020 – but this was significantly reduced as a result of the impact of COVID-19, having originally been set at a jaw-dropping £184m. The UK's Information Commissioner Elizabeth Denham was quoted as saying, 'When organisations take poor decisions around people's personal data, that can have a real impact on people's lives. The law now gives us the tools to encourage businesses to make better decisions about data, including investing in up-to-date security.'[22]

Large companies will always be targets for hackers because of the potential high-value rewards. While smaller companies are generally not so much of a target, less stringent security practices have the potential to make them more vulnerable. A breach or failure in security in a small company could be damaging enough to force it out of business.

Website security isn't only about protecting customer data. As soon as a website vulnerability has been identified, there's usually a gold rush by hackers to exploit it with details shared across the darker corners

---

22 I Lunden, 'UK's ICO reduces British Airways data breach fine to £20m, after originally setting it at £184m', TechCrunch, 2020, https://techcrunch.com/2020/10/16/uks-ico-downgrades-british-airways-data-breach-fine-to-20m-after-originally-setting-it-at-184m

of the internet. While the initial intent may not be directly malicious towards your business, the impact causes downtime and disruption, not to mention the potential for significant brand damage.

Scalability

A key consideration with a technology platform is its ability to grow and scale alongside your business as its needs inevitably evolve. Think about how your strategy will change over the years to come. Will you introduce eCommerce? What about product subscriptions? Will the current technology support an exponential growth in your user base?

The underlying architecture of different systems means that some will scale better than others. Adding new functionality should be supported by your chosen technology, and you need to be confident that the platform's own development roadmap is progressive, built on mainstream frameworks that are continually improving over time.

Training

Running multiple types of websites on different platforms can result in you having to provide training on all of them. Consolidating your website to a single platform can save significant costs by providing a consistent approach to training your team to use its features.

Hosting

Having settled on a technology platform, you need to decide how this will be hosted. Hosting is a critical part of your technology infrastructure, sharing the first line of defence against attackers and playing a crucial part in the overall experience enjoyed by your website visitors.

Few websites have a consistent level of traffic throughout the year, so being able to scale resources up and down to reflect demand can save on infrastructure costs and help play your part in not squandering the energy required to power and support your website. Cloud hosting these days is efficient and scalable, is distributed around the world and uses shared hardware, eliminating many of the single points of failure associated with more traditional dedicated servers.

The best hosting environment for your website will depend on a number of factors such as:

- Traffic

- Types of content (eg video or streaming)

- Audience locations

- Integrations with other systems

Providers such as Google Cloud and Amazon Web Services offer a plethora of hosting services. Most websites will rely on a combination of products, although usually from within the same vendor suite to maximise compatibility and scale.

Summary

Websites are inherently technology-based projects. When you can identify the software tools you're currently using in your business and how they fit together, you'll be well on the way to ensuring technology will be supportive and productive for you. This involves knowing the shortcomings of your technology stack – all the digital platforms, applications and services you use to run your business – before you make a commitment to a particular platform or service for your website.

You'll often find different software features overlap with those found in other platforms, or can even be combined into a single system. Be careful about adopting multiple systems and not getting the full value from them, or having several platforms that cause confusion over which is responsible for what.

As you consider the internal processes your website will support, you're likely to develop a feel for the relevant technology it needs to be able to connect with to do so. Your website technology choices should give you the freedom to integrate with other software and use the improved connectivity to grow your business.

Actions

Using your learnings from this chapter, look at some of the processes you've identified as being impacted by the website. Do you need to speak with your IT department to learn about other projects that might be happening across the business? How can technology best support your processes?

Make a list of your current technology stack. By sharing this with an agency, you ensure the people you are working with are better placed to make recommendations that capitalise on your existing technology choices, opening up new routes for implementation or adding to your digital strategy. An audit of your tech stack could reveal under-used platforms and provide opportunities to save money and streamline performance.

Who are your technology providers? Do you know who you need to contact if you have a problem? I've often been alarmed by companies that have struggled to identify the holder of their greatest digital assets, such as their domain registrar or website hosting provider.

How do your colleagues and customers feel about the technology used in the business? Do they use it in the way it was originally intended? Or have they found convenient workarounds because it doesn't fit their needs accurately?

Consider whether your existing technology is a help or a hindrance. What would you change? What would you miss if it was removed?

Look at how current your technology is. Is it secure? How regularly is it updated and does it adequately protect your assets?

7
Actions And Audience

'We don't make money when we sell things.
We make money when we help customers make
purchase decisions.'
  —Jeff Bezos, Amazon founder

So far in our DISTANCE method, we've spent a lot of time thinking about what *we* as website owners want to get from the website. For a website project to be successful, though, we also need give weighty consideration to those people visiting the site, as it's their actions that will ultimately determine whether our goals for the site will be met. There are too many companies pushing messages based on what they *think* their audience wants (or worse, what they want to tell them), rather than what they *actually* want.

In this chapter, I'll talk about how you might define your audiences and explore the different types of actions that you and they will want to take if they're to get value from your website. Of course, this has much wider benefits for your business; it isn't restricted to your website, but extends to your wider sales, marketing and product development activities.

Although this chapter is focused on your audience, as we saw in Chapter 4 when we talked about internal process, considering your calls to action allows you to design part of your business and how customers will experience it. A call to action triggers a process, regardless of whether it's automated or not, and yet it's one of the most overlooked aspects of a website. It's as simple as 'if you don't ask, you won't get' and will make the difference between driving actions and opening conversations, and visitors to your site finding themselves at a dead end and having to turn around.

Establishing an audience

Understanding your audiences is crucial to being able to create the right messages and adopt a clear position in your market and the eyes of your potential customers. Without knowing your audience, you won't know what they care about, what to say to them or how to say it.

Knowing your audience won't just make a difference with your website messaging. When all your different customer touchpoints join together with a consistent approach and message, your brand will become stronger. Your audience will grow and join you on the journey, rewarding you with their trust and allowing you in to not only their inboxes, but their lives.

As Seth Godin said in a blog post entitled 'Permission Marketing', 'Real permission works like this: if you stop showing up, people complain, they ask where you went.'[23] He goes on to say that 'marketing is the privilege (not the right) of delivering anticipated, personal and relevant messages to people who actually want to get them'. Earning the trust of your audience won't happen if you send them irrelevant messages.

Demographics

Truly knowing your audience is difficult. Most company leaders are able to create broad segments from their target audiences, demographics being an obvious way to do this using characteristics such as age or gender, often supplemented with socio-economic attributes like education, income or location. The problem with demographics is they are generalisations.

---

23   S Godin, 'Permission marketing', seths.blog, 2008, https://seths. blog/2008/01/permission-mark

That's not to say they're not valid. Demographics give us a way to monitor broad trends and allow us to measure societal change that might reflect the state of economic or cultural norms. But they're just one source of data that can usually be obtained without too much research. You're going to have to dig deeper to support your positioning and content.

Psychographics

If demographics explain *who* your audience is made up of, psychographics will help you move away from the hard facts and learn about what matters to them. Psychographics include personal attributes like habits, interests and values; the things that motivate, frustrate or anger them; and what ultimately drives them into action.

When you know what your audience's psychographic attributes are, you're able to frame the conversation you want to have with them. A conversation with a thirty-five-year-old woman (the demographic) could take any form, but a conversation with that same person when you know she has an interest in environmental issues to protect the planet for the future benefit of her young children would be vastly different (psychographics). If you then learn that she spends time on Facebook, telling her friends about the electric car she's bought and promoting how her sustainable living choices will minimise her carbon footprint – well, you get the picture.

This information is powerful. The more detailed a picture of your audience you can build, the more targeted and accurate your messaging can be.

Using personas

Personas are a common way to define audience segments using a combination of demographics and psychographics. In fact, we created a persona above with the example of the thirty-five-year-old woman promoting sustainable living and her electric car. Individual personas are often given personal names to bring them to life and may even be identified through a photograph to help people picture who they're trying to reach.

It's useful to know that 'Jane' has a university education, earns a salary of £60,000 a year and has developed a keen interest in environmental issues since becoming a parent. But this doesn't go into the detail of what her particular pain points are and what she would truly value from the product or service you can offer her.

For your audience to take action, they need to recognise their problems in your content. In fact, I'd go as far as saying you need to describe their frustrations better than they can and articulate distinct benefits you can bring to their lives. A distinct benefit isn't a generic one such as saving time or reducing plastic packaging. We all likely want these benefits. They're not compelling enough alone for people to take action. It's not about making something 'simpler', but going an extra layer below these generalisations.

Connecting with your audience

In addition to knowing *who* people in your audience are, it can also be helpful to understand how they *feel*. There can be a time and a place for certain messages, so understanding people's emotional feelings as they spend time on your website can make for a smoother visitor journey.

Empathy maps

The empathy map was created by visual thinker Dave Gray to help teams develop a deep shared understanding and empathy for other people.[24] It can be used for lots of different purposes, but one of its common applications is to enhance customer experience. Again, this experience doesn't need to be limited to your website, but can be easily applied to other areas or customer touchpoints across your business.

---

24   D Gray, 'Empathy map', Gamestorming, 2017, https://gamestorming. com/empathy-mapping. Also D Gray, *Gamestorming: A playbook for innovators, rulebreakers, and changemakers* (O'Reilly Media, 2010)

The skill with empathy mapping isn't about guessing at people's frustrations and ambitions, but actually putting yourself in someone else's shoes and thinking about how you (and they) might react under a given set of circumstances. Empathy maps have taken various formats over the years, but essentially, they pose questions about what people see, think, feel and do. They incorporate the language people might hear, from whom and how it might influence them. How do people's attitudes change through their experience and how will this be influenced by things like the device they're using or the location they're in? What are the comparisons they make with other products or your competitors?

Empathy maps allow you to capture both internal and external influences on people's behaviour and ensure your thinking and the way you design your website are centred around the hopes and fears of your users at all times. To do this effectively, you need to ask yourself:

- Who are you empathising with? Who do you want to understand? What is their situation? What is their role in this situation?

- What does this person do? What do they need to do differently? What do they need to get done? What decisions will this involve? How will you know when they're successful?

- What does this person see in their marketplace? Their environment? In what others are saying and doing? What are they studying?

- What have you heard them say? What can you imagine them saying?

- What are they doing today? What can you imagine them doing? What behaviour have you observed?

- What are they hearing from their colleagues? Their friends? What are they hearing second hand?

- What do they feel? What are their **pains**: fears, frustrations and anxieties? What are their **gains**: wants, needs, hopes and dreams?

You can access the original empathy map at https://medium.com/the-xplane-collection/updated-empathy-map-canvas-46df22df3c8a

What do people need to achieve?

The phrase 'top tasks' and the method behind it were coined by Gerry McGovern in his 2018 book, *Top Tasks: A how-to guide*.[25] He explains that top tasks are the most important things your customers need to do when they're on your website, and they exist in any environment or general activity, be that buying

---

25 G McGovern, *Top Tasks: A how-to guide* (Silver Beach, 2018), https://gerrymcgovern.com/books/top-tasks-a-how-to-guide

a car, looking for information from a local council or researching information about healthcare. When these goals are well served, your organisation's goals will be reached more quickly as you'll provide a better customer experience.

How do you know what your audience's top tasks are? It all comes back to understanding the world your customer lives in (which can include internal stakeholders in larger websites) by looking at data and real-world experience. Having run Top Task Identification Projects for over fifteen years, McGovern says he typically finds an inverse relationship between what companies care about and what the customer cares about. In other words, company leaders are far happier to talk about their business than spend the time to understand and address the needs of their audience first.

User stories

The idea of user stories originates from a practice called agile software development (there's more about agile in Chapter 10). While a website build project won't necessarily follow an agile development approach, I particularly like the concept of user stories because they focus on user-centred outcomes while helping to define technical requirements and features for your website. Having an understanding of your audience through the personas you've explored, and then knowing the tasks they want to complete, you can justify and prioritise the inclusion of a particular feature on the website based on *what the user needs to achieve.*

A user story is simply:

'As a [persona], I want to… so that…'

If we think back to the persona we created earlier, it might read something like this:

'As Jane (a forty-year-old mum with an interest in reducing my carbon footprint), I want to be able to buy environmentally friendly baby products on a monthly subscription that I can manage online so that I don't end up with unwanted products that could go to waste.'

Like top tasks, user stories can be relevant to internal audiences as much as external, and there are several benefits to working with them, some of which are specific to the agile approach to project management which we'll cover later on in the book. From an audience and scope-planning perspective, the customer-centric thinking that goes into user stories encourages collaboration across departments and allows you to explore different stories for different personas, each of which can spin off several subtasks that enable you to meet the demands of your audience and add value, creating a great experience.

Retaining trust

While segmenting your audience and creating a picture of how they feel is valuable intelligence to support your business, one of the most crucial elements of business today is transparency. It's not good enough to simply talk the talk; consumers have grown to be savvier and more cynical when it comes to interpreting marketing messages, and transparency is one of the attributes most demanded from businesses.

In 2017, the annual Earned Brand report from global communications agency Edelman found that one in two people were 'belief-driven buyers'.[26] This increased to two in three the following year. These were people who would choose, switch, avoid or boycott a brand based on its stand on societal issues.

We've witnessed brands taking public positions on global issues such as climate and race. The growing belief that business should be a force for good has been reflected in the rise of the B Corps movement, which saw an increase from 82 companies certified in 2006 to over 3,500 today across 70 countries.[27] The B Corps governing body found that 76% of the UK public think business has a responsibility to protect

26   Edelman, 'Brands take a stand', Edelman Earned Brand, 2018, www.edelman.com/sites/g/files/aatuss191/files/2018-10/2018_Edelman_Earned_Brand_Global_Report.pdf
27   Certified B Corporation, 'About B Corps', bcorporation.net, no date, https://bcorporation.net/faq-categories/about-b-corps

the environment and the majority favour brands that are doing good in the world.[28]

This new level of brand activism is being pushed by audiences whose expectations are rising, with their endorsements ultimately made through their wallets. It's no longer good enough to simply identify your audience and say what they want to hear; it's vital to share their values and beliefs if they're going to appear in any of your audience segments for any length of time.

Mapping the customer journey

So far in this chapter, we've looked at the importance of identifying your audiences, how they feel and what matters to them. As we move into the next section of the chapter where we think about relevant calls to action, we'll start to build a picture of your customer's journey. Seeing things from your customer's perspective is critical to achieving success with your website, and other aspects of your marketing and wider methods of doing business.

As digital channels have proliferated, the customer journey has become far more complex. Most customer journeys will include your website, but in the

---

28 Certified B Corporation, 'Our economic "operating system" needs upgrading', bcorporation.net, no date, https://bcorporation.uk/system-upgrade

'omnichannel' world we live in, you also need to consider social media, email and third-party reviews as a minimum. Factoring in personal experiences such as live chat and face-to-face contact is a valuable part of the journey, but what a lot of people don't realise is that this is a journey without a destination. There's no longer a linear path to purchase from point A to point B. People are looking at different types of information across the web, crucially with different intents at each point as they build up a picture of your brand, products or services.

As people think about their buying decisions, they turn to their devices for immediate answers to ensure their requirements will be met. This might result in them making multiple searches, watching videos or listening to podcasts and reading reviews, so they can easily have hundreds of 'micro-interactions' with your brand along the way to becoming a customer, and even once they've become a customer.

It's important to measure these micro-interactions and understand their impact on your customers, and how that reflects on progress towards your goals. Which ones make or break the journey? Which ones excite or disappoint? Which ones cause you to lose people who drop out and choose a different path? You can't control the overall experience customers have across your different channels, but having a strategy that presents relevant calls to action when people next engage with you can move their intent to the next stage.

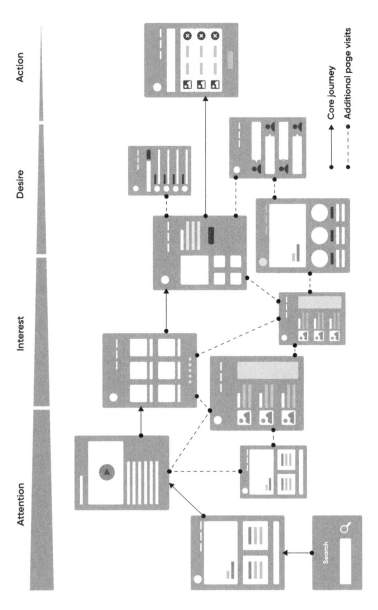

A real-word customer journey (page layout graphics used with kind permission of uxkits.com)

Calls to action

Having captured the attention of your audience, you're going to need to give them some guidance to direct them to what it is you can offer them. This is where calls to action come in. You need your audience to take a decisive step, ideally moving both you and them towards a win-win situation.

An influential usability test that explored the relationship between a user's first click on a website and their eventual success in completing an entire task shows just how important calls to action are. The study found that if the first click was correct, the likelihood of the task being completed was 87%. Compare this with visits where the first click was incorrect, and the success rate plummeted to just 46%. Participants were almost twice as likely to be successful in achieving their goal if their first click was the correct one.[29]

There are dozens of possible calls to action, but the vast majority revolve around a key action you want people to be able to take to move a conversation to the next stage or advance them through your sales funnel. I've listed some of the most common 'trigger words' below, but don't think of these as the call to action itself. Identifying which ones will be relevant to you is just the start point, helping you to determine what

29 B Bailey, 'FirstClick usability testing', Web Usability.com, 2013, http://webusability.com/firstclick-usability-testing

should happen next, and the type and tone of content you require to support it.

You might want to encourage your website visitors to:

- Download

- Subscribe

- Buy

- Express interest

- Register

- Share

- Trial

- Search

- Explore

- Learn

- Start

These calls to action will most likely be buttons on your website so they stand out to your visitors, clearly identifiable as a signpost to guide them towards their end goal. There's no reason why standard links can't be calls to action, but these generally aren't as visually strong and can be easily overlooked.

Notice with each of the trigger words that I've not included the word 'click'. Click might be the physical action you want someone to take, but it's bland and doesn't direct the visitor towards their ultimate goal. It offers no suggestion of what might happen next, and with the wide range of devices people are using, not everyone clicks these days, either.

Depending on the type of page you're creating, it might be that you need to include the same call to action multiple times. Just because you've added a button to the page doesn't mean people will see it or have seen enough information at that stage to act on it. A high-performing landing page, for example, will likely feature several buttons with slight variations of text. As visitors scroll down the page and their understanding of your product or service grows, the text you use in the call to action may differ or become more persuasive.

Strengthening calls to action

The language you use in calls to action should influence and motivate people to take that action. People don't want to miss out or associate themselves with a negative state, and let's be honest, you have sales targets to meet, too.

There are lots of ways to strengthen calls to action, which might include:

- Creating urgency
- Thinking like the customer

- Reminding visitors of a goal they might have (eg 'Start your journey today')

- Giving the customer control (eg 'Activate your discount now')

- Joining others (social proof that others are using the product as well)

- Demonstrating exclusivity

- Following established convention (eg 'What Amazon does'), but use with caution

- Avoiding questions (unless there's a negative answer)

All of these are legitimate ways to encourage people into action, but in reality, a call to action can be seen as coercing people, or worse, attempting to manipulate their behaviour. It's one thing to take the time to build trust and loyalty, and quite another to trick people into actions they may later regret.

Dark patterns

Everything on the internet is fighting for your attention: share buttons, news (and fake news), social media memes, that special offer price that always ends with a 7 and, of course, your legitimate attempts to grow your business. With all this noise, online design trickery known as dark patterns have emerged as methods to dupe people into actions they might not have meant to take. There's even a website and Twitter account carrying a 'Hall of Shame' of companies using questionable design techniques that deliberately create confusion. Even though many marketing teams are coming under increasing pressure to meet the targets and goals set by senior management, dark patterns are to be avoided.

I wonder how many of you have unwittingly signed up to an Amazon Prime account because it offered you free delivery. I imagine quite a few, and in 2019, the UK's Advertising Standards Authority ruled the ad during Amazon's checkout process was misleading.[30] The primary call to action button on the page included the text 'Order Now with Prime' adjacent to 'Continue with FREE one-day delivery, pay later'. The option to continue to the checkout without signing up for the trial was small, faint in colour and significantly less prominent, and placed in a position which could easily be missed by consumers.

As the quote at the head of the chapter shows, Amazon founder Jeff Bezos knows that by helping people to make buying decisions, his company makes money. But the method of doing so in this example was clearly dubious. The risks from this approach might be outweighed by the fact that so many people still enjoy the benefits of selection, price and convenience

---

30   ASA, 'ASA ruling on Amazon Europe Core Sarl', ASA.org.uk, 2019,
     www.asa.org.uk/rulings/amazon-europe-core-sarl-G19-1021643.html

147

Amazon provides, but it's a risk not all companies can afford to take.

Amazon isn't alone, though. Booking.com has urgency messages splashed all over the place which can easily blend into your subconscious and influence your decision making. Ryanair has been known to trick visitors into opting-in to its own insurance when booking a flight, and there's an increasing trend on eCommerce sites for showing how many people are viewing a product at the same time you are.

There's little argument that dark patterns work at the point they're implemented, but there are far more legitimate and effective routes to maximising your calls to action that build longer-term brand value to your offer. Engaging in dark patterns can result in a customer backlash, increased costs in customer service and negative reviews, meaning the long-term damage will far outweigh any short-term gains.

Summary

In this chapter, we've looked at why segmenting your audiences into well-defined groups is so important and considered some techniques for doing so. Your audiences should feed into your strategy and will have a pivotal impact on your content – not just on your website, but across all your channels.

Of course, those channels themselves are also defined by your audience.

Calls to action are the equivalent of saying, 'Shall we talk about it?' You're encouraging the next step in a remote conversation. Missing calls to action are the equivalent of your site visitors walking into a shop and being ignored by the assistant. Without the inter-action, visitors are left to their own devices to find things out for themselves, with you unable to shape the direction or influence the decisions they take.

Of course, audiences change. Your customers might fundamentally be the same people, but their interests, habits and values can change over time, so it's vital to recognise this by collecting and reviewing data in your business to keep up with demands and expectations.

As you build your audiences, you're building trust, so the number-one rule is to show them respect and reward them with content that's valuable and doesn't spam their inbox or trick them into something they might later regret. The court of public opinion can lead to PR disasters with damaging reviews and social media posts that can be difficult to recover from.

Actions

Using your learnings from this chapter, make a list of your core audiences. You can start with either demographics or psychographics, but explore how you can narrow this list down as much as possible. The more focused your messaging is to your audiences, the more likely it is to resonate with them. If you have a mailing list already, look at how well this is segmented into specific audience groups.

Review the calls to action on your website. Does every page have one? Is it relevant? A page without a call to action is potentially a dead end for website visitors and won't support lead generation.

Consider running usability tests on your website, such as a First Click or 5-Second Test. A First Click Test is easily set by asking someone where they would click on a page on your website to complete a simple task. Measure where they click and how long it takes them to make their choice. A 5-Second Test can be completed by showing someone a page for 5 seconds and them asking them about what they saw. Did they spot the calls to action?

Visit your website having completed an empathy map or explored a list of top tasks for one of your audience segments. How does the website make you feel? Does it provide an answer to your problem and support your intent at that point in time? What can you offer visitors to your website in exchange for learning something about them? Provide them with something valuable to capture not only their email address, but perhaps two or three other pieces of information that can help you better understand them and their likely intent.

Measure your audiences and their actions with formal usability testing or data tools such as Google Analytics so you can improve performance. How can you build stronger relationships with customers, even when you're offering more services online? How can you remain available rather than leave customers feeling disconnected?

8
Normalising A Digital Culture

'The world as we have created it is a process of our thinking. It cannot be changed without changing our thinking.'
—Albert Einstein

While a new website may take centre stage, or at least play a significant role in how you present your organisation online, if your site is to Go the DISTANCE, it needs to be set against an organisational culture that integrates digital technology with collaborative thinking across the business. For many companies, this represents an ongoing cultural adaptation more widely known as digital transformation, but there's much more to this than simply introducing new technology.

Digital transformation is about having an awareness of and being able to identify opportunities for digital technology to improve the way your organisation functions, both internally and externally. Despite the suggestion of technology driving the process of digital transformation, the case for it is fundamentally about people. Internally, for people to have meaning in their work and make an impact in their jobs or their communities, they need the best tools that are designed for their workflows and the way they work. Externally, it's about being able to meet the needs of your customers on their terms, wherever they happen to be on their buying journey with you.

Despite the rise of disruptor businesses in the digital space such as Airbnb, Uber and Stripe, for many companies, their digital journeys were still at a relatively early stage two decades into the twenty-first century. But the impact of the global lockdowns due to COVID-19 meant digital transformation came into sharp focus on their strategic agendas.

Take Primark as an example. With no online eCommerce operation, its monthly revenue plummeted from £650m to zero as its stores were closed during lockdown and it had no alternative sales channels for its products.[31] Granted, these were exceptional circumstances and few would have predicted such a dramatic

---

31 E Jahshan, 'Primark's monthly sales nosedive from £650m to zero', *Retail Gazette*, 2020, www.retailgazette.co.uk/blog/2020/04/primarks-monthly-sales-nosedive-from-650m-to-zero

shutdown of society, but by having a solid digital operation in place, Primark could potentially have seen an increase in its revenue as customers turned to shopping online, rather than such a significant decline.

The enforced shift to remote working for many companies during the pandemic also accelerated the need for digital transformation. The companies that found this switch relatively painless were already using online tools and cloud-based software, and for those that were less well prepared, the likely increase in people wanting greater flexibility in how and where they work will have had a significant impact on their technology choices and cultural development going forwards.

Clearly, digital transformation goes well beyond your website, and as an entire topic, it extends beyond the scope of this book. But thinking digitally, collaborating across teams and departments, and identifying new opportunities for technology to improve performance will enable you to use your website in such a way that it becomes a valuable asset and not simply a marketing tool.

Successful digital transformation

Digital transformation has been notoriously challenging for companies to succeed at. Depending on where you look, figures suggest anywhere from just 5–30% of so-called transformations are successful. Because of this low success rate, an understanding of how your organisation is adapting and pursuing digital transformation is crucial when you're planning a new website. Although your website is far from the be all and end all with digital transformation, in most cases it will form a central point in your customer's journey, so at least understanding how it will be used is vital to the planning and build stages.

Not everyone likes the term 'digital transformation'. As we saw in Chapter 4, such a great scale of change can feel insurmountable and curtail progress towards the desired goal. Referring back to my podcast interview with Richard Godfrey, he argues that companies themselves don't need to transform, but simply become more efficient in their use of technology while putting human needs at the core of the process.

Despite this view, the phrase 'digital transformation' is widely recognised and accepted. Following several years of research, in 2018, McKinsey identified a set of five factors that are fundamental to successful digital transformations.[32] These are:

- Having the right digital-savvy leaders in place

- Building capabilities for the workforce of the future

---

32 McKinsey & Company, 'Survey: Unlocking success in digital transformations', mckinsey.com, 2018, www.mckinsey.com/ business-functions/organization/our-insights/unlocking-success-in-digital-transformations

- Empowering people to work in new ways

- Giving day-to-day tools a digital upgrade

- Communicating frequently via traditional and digital methods

These points all seem fairly obvious, but introducing them into an existing way of being is never easy, especially where people may be fearful of how they'll impact on their current roles. My Go the DISTANCE method doesn't seek to drive organisational change as part of your website build, but to highlight the importance of a digital-led culture that can adapt to internal and external human demands and capitalise on new opportunities for growth.

What is culture?

Like strategy, culture is another word from the corporate lexicon that is widely misused and misunderstood. Culture can't be seen or implemented, but is an incredibly powerful tool that sets expectations around how people perform, ultimately bringing together a set of beliefs and values to create a winning team.

Unlike strategy, the culture in your business cannot be easily replicated by others. Culture is often the reason why different teams achieve varying levels of performance when in reality, they all have exactly the same potential. Unfortunately, with culture inextricably linked to people's collective (and therefore individual) behaviour, it can be hard to change. Change it must, though, if you're to take advantage of how digital influences people's individual behaviours and the wider changes seen across society.

Culture is essentially the environment in which things get done. Your goals and strategy will be achieved when the people delivering them can work effectively, both individually and as part of a team, each person understanding their role and the responsibilities placed upon them in pursuit of a common purpose they believe in. Millennials and younger generations in particular look for meaning in their work and want to join organisations that have a purpose and mission beyond profit, often giving this importance over and above the salary on offer.

Strong cultures begin with leadership. Normalising digital behaviours at this stage of the DISTANCE process is all about setting the scene and creating an environment for successful outcomes that will enable you to reach your goals and objectives. While you may not carry responsibility for leading a team in your role, I imagine at least you're responsible for delivering the strategy, and that means being able to influence and coach others while leading by example.

For culture to be effective, it must be understood by everybody. If it isn't, individual behaviours will pull in different directions and personal motivations can take hold, compromising the performance and rewards of the team or organisation. Having clarity on people's views and beliefs is essential to support your strategy and achieve your chosen outcomes.

What is a digital culture?

Digital culture is a state of mind, not simply keeping up by rolling out the latest computer hardware, website or CRM platform. As we've seen throughout this book, 'digital' covers a broad spectrum; deploying technology or pursuing elements of your strategy in isolation doesn't enable new ways of working or delivering value.

As Millennials have worked their way up the career ladder, their personal experiences and habits have heavily influenced the workplace and digital culture in particular. They've grown up with technology, enjoying real-time and continuous communication through social media and apps like Slack and Whats-App. They've had the benefit of flexible working and often access to more modern devices than many businesses and organisations, especially those in the public sector. They've had the technology and the time to trial different products and services, typically at no cost and with no risk. As they rise up the ranks into decision-making roles, they can't then be put in a position that leaves them feeling constrained by internal policy and outdated thinking.

The fusing of technology, innovation and culture is driving solutions that are fundamentally changing the products companies are selling, the way they're sold and how companies deliver value to their customers. In some cases, entirely new models and revenue streams are being developed, transforming the future of businesses as they continually adapt to changing demands. With application programming interfaces (APIs) that allow different systems and services to talk to each other, IoT devices, and now the rapid growth in AI and ML, websites and web-based applications have the potential to do and offer so much more to users than simply being a means of contact or to showcase your latest corporate video.

General Electric, Rolls-Royce and other manufacturers are no longer simply selling jet-engines; they're now selling uptime and reliability. A customer needs a jet-engine to power their aeroplane, but what they really want (and value) is reliability, performance and efficiency that allows them to maximise operational capacity. Incorporating sensors into each engine allows remote maintenance and monitoring, optimising service routines and maximising efficiency and safety.

Global lift and escalator manufacturer Schindler has pursued a similar strategy, collecting over 200m data points as it moves a billion people every day. Its products and services have been repackaged into long-term solutions, completely changing the nature of what it sells. This ability to gather and monitor data as its products are used allows Schindler to add value through the entire product lifecycle, react to failures and anticipate service issues, even identifying parts that need to be replaced – all in real time.

Electronics giant Philips is another example where a physical product has been successfully digitised. People need to light their buildings and premises, and while it is lightbulbs that provide this, a digital platform has enabled Philips to develop a fully integrated Lighting as a Service product, reducing cost, maintenance and environmental impact.

Cars are being sold by subscription these days. Jaguar Land Rover and Volvo are two examples of manufacturers offering a monthly subscription providing all-inclusive car ownership with the flexibility to easily change your model. You can pause your subscription if your needs change, and even work your way around the entire range of models every few months at no added cost. This is a step change away from the typical large cash outlay and long-term commitment normally required for owning a car.

Subscriptions are a logical choice for product extension strategies. People don't want ownership and liability anymore; they want convenience, simplicity and added value. The subscription model provides recurring revenue and the opportunity to keep learning more about your customers through the product lifecycle, which in turn enables you to improve the service you provide them with.

These examples don't just illustrate how creative and iterative thinking can develop new revenue streams and business opportunities. Investment in platforms and assets such as these creates new intellectual property that can further reinforce your market position and the ability to nurture relationships with customers while attracting and retaining talent within your team. Research from PwC suggests that customers are the most powerful disruptive force facing business, with 86% of CEOs believing their customers will demand more from their products over the next five years.[33]

Of course, this type of progress doesn't emanate from a single individual. It takes collaboration across departments and even entire organisations, openness to ideas and permission to ~~fail~~ learn from every experience. Furthermore, it takes technically savvy leadership to recognise new opportunities, the impact of changing markets and how technology can be applied for human benefit.

---

33 PwC Global, 'The CEO agenda', pwc.com, no date, www.pwc.com/gx/en/ceo-agenda/pulse/the-disruptors.html

Digital leadership

Culture is defined by leadership and the digital leader is tasked with creating an environment that brings together technical skills, process (which in most cases will revolve around people) and technology. Digital leaders need to bring with them attributes that encourage new ideas and experimentation, collaboration and support for continual learning. Their focus should be on using data to build assets that create value, support scale and deliver a competitive edge. It's important for customers' needs to be placed at the heart of these developments.

Google has a saying in its philosophy: 'Focus on the user and all else will follow'.[34] While this is true, your business is also a user of technology and the systems and processes you put in place, so it's important not to overlook your own needs if your digital transformation is to be a success.

Everything in digital is connected, so it makes natural sense that digital leaders should be creating their own equivalent connections, both internally and through external partnerships. Not only can this reveal new ideas and approaches to deliver value and improve efficiency, but it also goes a long way to uniting disparate teams and achieving buy-in from across the organisation.

---

34 Google, 'Ten things we know to be true', Google.com, no date, www.google.com/about/philosophy.html

Leaders need to be entrepreneurial in their approach, and when appropriate, treat digital projects like startup businesses in their own right. *Design thinking* is an iterative approach developed by the Interaction Design Foundation that can be used to challenge assumptions, reframe problems in human-centric ways and create innovative solutions to tackle these problems.[35] Ultimately, this leads to a prototype that can be tested in the wild with the lessons learned applied as the problem and potential solution are refined.

It's unlikely every digital campaign, product or service will be perfect first time. Much is said about digital products being allowed to fail and how failing fast encourages quicker innovation. Thomas Edison famously said that he didn't fail, he just found 10,000 ways that didn't work, and I much prefer this more optimistic perspective than considering failures.

It is true whether you're building a product or running an ad campaign, you'll invariably find out much more quickly what doesn't work than what does. The advantage with digital products or campaigns is that you're not committed to a minimum run of thousands of units so you can quickly course correct or rectify mistakes, often without having incurred huge upfront costs. Being prepared to experiment in a way

---

35   R Friis Dam and T Yu Siang, 'What is design thinking and why is it so popular?', Interaction Design Foundation, no date, www.interaction-design.org/literature/topics/design-thinking

that carries the risk of mistakes or failures can be an awkward shift for more traditional organisations, but it feeds and shapes internal knowledge. Taking the view of being prolific rather than perfect may carry risk, but it can also bring with it the advantage of being first to market and the potential to disrupt the status quo.

Digital teams

A digital culture starts at leadership level, but it's vital that this culture extends into teams working at every level. But in many companies, internal teams are often found operating in silos with limited communication between them.

It once made sense to group people together with colleagues from their own team; marketing, finance, HR and operations would have occupied their own parts of the building and been like ships passing in the night – aware of each other, occasionally acknowledging one another's existence, but unsure about the true heading or challenges they face. As digital impacts teams across the business, the companies undergoing a successful digital transformation are breaking down these silos for the benefit of customers and internal teams.

Let's take a product example. There might be a team that oversees production, but it's the customer-service team that deals with any problems or issues experienced by customers. A customer may contact your customer-service team for support or share their disappointment on social media, which might be managed by your marketing team. Without joining these touchpoints together, you risk that customer feedback going to the marketing team instead of the product team, or the product team sharing improvements with the marketing team to update the website, but failing to inform the customer-service team. Processes become disjointed, inefficient and raise the chance of customers having a poor experience. Furthermore, any attempts to scale without addressing these inefficiencies can be met with even greater inefficiency, low morale, potentially chaos and ultimately failure.

Similar examples can be found with the need to create content. Every company is in the publishing business these days and we'll see in the next chapter the importance of having a clear plan and structure for creating content.

While working with a law firm, my team and I could see that visitors were asking technical questions around various points of law to solicitors, but these weren't being shared back to the marketing team members who were responsible for the website. The solicitors were unaware that the answers to these questions would have made fantastic content to aid search engine rankings on the website or social media posts, as in all likelihood, other potential clients would have similar, if not the same, questions.

These frequently asked questions could also have been packaged into an automated onboarding process for when a client first instructs a solicitor to act on their behalf. This would have created a distinctive and positive experience from the outset, saving valuable time by avoiding the need for these questions to be repeatedly answered in emails or opening discussions.

Relevant content that answers at least some of your visitors' questions demonstrates to them that you understand their needs and concerns, and reinforces your customers' belief that yours is the company that can resolve them. I'm sure we've all experienced buyers' remorse: that moment you briefly wonder whether you've made the right buying decision. By immediately countering that remorse, you can go a long way to providing peace of mind and strengthening your brand.

It's everyone's responsibility across your business to be listening and looking out for opportunities to create content, support problem solving and improve the customer experience. We've all likely heard the saying 'You can't see the wood for the trees'; teams sometimes need an external perspective to see challenges and solutions from a different angle. And to do that, they need to move away from the silo mentality.

Silos can be broken down by:

- Creating shared goals across departments or teams that are aligned with organisational-level goals

- Ensuring goals within individual departments are directly related to the overall company vision

- Educating and training people from different teams together

- Using collaborative tools

- Enabling regular communications with the right people around the table

Breaking down the silos within your organisation is an important step to helping people access the information they need to do their job. We've already talked about the impact Millennials have had on workplace culture; this group of people are perfectly comfortable with sharing their lives online, so they expect to be able to easily find information without it being trapped in a senior manager's inbox.

Building shared platforms such as a wiki or using collaborative workspace tools like Monday.com, Asana or Slack can aid the creation of communities or subgroups with supporting processes to document vital information or publish data to shared locations in the cloud. This not only removes the threat from poor communication, but also helps to develop the open and collaborative environment where people have all they need to do their best work.

Digital skills

Having the right people in the right seats is vital if you're to achieve your goals and fulfil your strategy. Digital skills have proliferated significantly over recent years and continue to do so as data collection and analysis become ever more important to business operations.

Simply giving people the right skills, though, isn't enough to get the most from them. They need to have the context in which to use those skills and understand why they're relevant to your organisation's wider purpose and objective. Upskilling your team will inevitably affect recruitment as well, so being able to make the right hiring decisions, both in terms of skills and cultural fit, will enormously impact on your ability to deliver and take action.

Digital has always had a relatively low barrier to entry for those new to the discipline. There are hundreds of 'gurus' offering online courses in digital, but it isn't something you simply learn and tick a box with. It's such a movable feast; the best performers will have a keenness to continually learn, often by creating their own side projects so they learn by doing, developing their first-hand experience at the same time. The strongest candidates will have a portfolio of work, and

169

potentially their own website from which to showcase it. As a minimum, they need to have views and opinions on relevant topics that they share and discuss on social media or in other online communities.

The exact combination of skills you need will depend on whether you intend to build your own in-house team or outsource part of the strategic delivery to freelancers or specialist agencies like A Digital. For the largest sites, teams will be led by a product manager and made up of developers or engineers who focus on a specific technology such as front-end coding languages like HTML, JavaScript and CSS; back-end languages like PHP or C#; or application frameworks such as Laravel, Vue.js or React. DevOps engineers (unifying software development and operations) will be responsible for things like testing, deployments and overseeing server infrastructure, while designers will focus on things like UX and user interaction. Content strategists may be introduced for the structural design of the site and information architecture (IA) (see Chapter 9 for more on IA).

While larger marketing teams will have a need for specialist roles, most small to medium-sized enterprises (SMEs) will have to build their teams with a diverse range of more generalist skills, which can include:

- Copywriting and storytelling
- Public relations

- SEO

- Using website CMSs

- Email marketing

- Automation

- Graphic design and UX

- Video and audio production

- Data analysis, including web analytics

- Commercial and strategic awareness

- Online advertising (social and search)

- Data protection and cybersecurity

Some company leaders may choose to specialise in their own aspects of marketing to ensure there is a core set of skills within the business. Others will choose to outsource some of these skills to an agency, often determined by whether a project is considered short-term versus those that drive cultural change and influence longer-term digital transformation, which need to be kept in-house.

Digital is never done

There's little doubt digital is a challenging place to be, and done is never truly done. 'Done' basically means starting the process over again with new insights and constraints. We'll talk more about execution in the final chapter of our DISTANCE method.

Digital is always evolving and demands that you and your team keep up with change, which is ultimately driven by your customers and the requirement for the business to evolve and become more efficient. While it's challenging, for me, this is part of the excitement as it fulfils my own purpose of solving problems with technology to improve people's lives.

There are few things more satisfying than when something simply works, especially when you might have expected it to be hard going. When you can tell something's been designed with care and attention to detail, the experience it provides is memorable and immensely satisfying. Make this the goal for your team: delighting your customers and consistently making things better in an environment that promotes people's best work.

Summary

If your site is to Go the DISTANCE, it needs to be set against an organisational culture that integrates digital technology with collaborative thinking. Digital transformation is fundamentally about people rather than technology. For people to have meaning in their work and make an impact, they need tools that are designed for their workflows and the way they work. Externally, your digital culture is about meeting the needs of your customers on their terms.

The fusing of technology, innovation and culture is fundamentally changing the products companies are selling and the way they're selling them. With the growth in APIs, IoT devices, AI and ML, websites and web-based applications have the potential to offer so much more to users.

Digital leaders need attributes that encourage new ideas and experimentation, collaboration and support for continual learning, focusing on using data to build assets that create value, support scale and deliver a competitive edge. Having the right people in the right seats is vital if you're to achieve your goals. And it's important for customers' needs to be placed at the heart of these developments.

Actions

Using your learnings from this chapter, create a cross-departmental team (that could be an individual) to unify silos and gather information about who does what. What opportunities come out of the conversations that take place?

What are your digital beliefs or values? Include your team to define what being creative, collaborative or 'digital' means to them.

Encourage new ideas across the business. You could create a 'labs' team responsible for innovation to test and experiment with new ideas and build a business case to launch them. This doesn't have to be a full-time department, but perhaps a regular meetup to discuss opportunities.

How does your environment facilitate collaborative working? Is the culture formal and risk-averse, or is there room for mistakes to be made and lessons learned? How can you empower individuals to perform to their best? Encourage people to take breaks from their screen and remind them human interaction is central to digital behaviours and team performance.

What are the skills you need to develop your digital offering? How will you build relationships with remote teams and contributors that keep ideas flowing and people engaged?

Determine the maturity of your internal skillset. Who can do what? What are the training needs? Which skills and activities are best kept in-house to support cultural change and enhancement? Will new roles be required?

9
Content

'High-quality web content that's useful, usable, and enjoyable is one of the greatest competitive advantages you can create for yourself online.'
—Kristina Halvorson, Content Strategist and author, *Content Strategy for the Web*

The content on your website is one of the most fundamental aspects of your planning process. Having come this far in the DISTANCE method and built up the other stages, you'll be in a good position to think about your content. You'll know what the data from your research has shown you, what your goals are going to be and how you're going to achieve them. You'll have considered the technology you'll use and the calls to action you want your visitors to pursue to meet both your and their goals. With the steps identified to ensure the right people are in the right seats, the next thing to address is your content.

Content is not just about writing the words for your website. Sarah Richards, founder of Content Design London, defined the term 'content design' while working for the UK Government Digital Service. With billions of pages on the internet, she argues that to do better than your competitors, you need smarter content, and this means not just limiting yourself to words. Data and research will identify what your customers actually need, which isn't always the same as what they say they want.[36]

Content breaks down into two stages; *content strategy* is the planning and development of what you're creating where and why. With a strategy agreed, it's possible to move on to *content production* that will fill your pages, traverse your marketing channels and support your overall UX.

Content is crucially important. Why would you need a website with no content? People searching on Google are looking for answers. They are looking for content that can help them solve a problem, make their lives easier or provide them with entertainment. With access to the world's information at their fingertips, they don't have to settle for anything less. Content allows people to move to the next stage of doing

---

36   S Richards, *Content Design* (Content Design London, 2017)

business with you, and without it, no other aspect of the DISTANCE method is possible.

Content is basically everything that sits within your website. It's like the furnishings inside a house that add character, warmth and comfort. It's a representative of your business greeting your visitors as they walk through the front door, setting the tone for who you are and what you want to be to your customers.

Content includes:

- Written copy

- Photography

- Video

- Charts and infographics

- Maps

- Live webinars and offline events

- Podcasts

- Downloadable PDF files or other documents

- Content 'pulled in' from other sources, which might include a Twitter feed, third-party news or press release services, or live share prices and investor data for public companies listed on the Stock Exchange

Few websites will achieve their goals with purely written content. Websites are far more informative and engaging when they feature multimedia elements that add personality and interactivity. But the real reason for including content beyond the written word is quite simple.

When web usability consultant Jakob Nielsen carried out research back in 1997 into how people 'read the web', his simple conclusion was: 'They don't'. He found that 79% of test users scanned any new page they came across, with only 16% reading the page word-for-word.[37] In 2008, following research by Harald Weinreich which was later abstracted by Nielsen, he concluded that visitors to an average web page had time to read at most 28% of the words during a visit, although closer to just 20% was more likely.[38]

Since 2008, most of us have contributed to the meteoric rise of social media platforms and our online behaviours have been hugely influenced by the growth of the mobile web. With so many more distractions competing for our attention, I can only imagine that if readers are still consuming 20% of your page content today, you're doing better than most.

---

37 J Nielsen, 'How users read on the web', Nielsen Norman Group, 1997, www.nngroup.com/articles/how-users-read-on-the-web
38 J Nielsen, 'How little do users read?', Nielsen Norman Group, 2008, www.nngroup.com/articles/how-little-do-users-read

Despite the low likelihood that people will read even a single page on your website in its entirety, strong copywriting is incredibly important. People shouldn't need to read your page word-for-word to understand your product or service, but the content they do read could make the difference between them taking action or deciding to return to their search results. Knowing the actions you'd like them to take is key to planning what your content will look like, how visitors flow through your website and how you can build a relationship with them.

Whatever combination of content you're planning for your site, it all needs to link together to deliver a clear and consistent message, build trust and be compelling enough to drive the actions you've already identified.

How to create great content

Great content builds trust and establishes your authority. But how can you achieve this if people aren't reading it?

Content can be designed as well as written and the UX that greets your visitors will affect the way your content is perceived. Fundamentally, content needs to be authentic. It needs to deliver on the promise of the headline or excerpt that attracted people in the first place, and it needs to be relevant to your audience.

Cheap-looking stock images, spelling mistakes or click-bait headlines all diminish the authenticity of your content, which immediately raises a question of trust. These attributes of an article or content piece are obvious and not only discourage people from reading your content, but seriously damage your brand. To add further insult to injury, companies producing this type of content often expect people to join their mailing list by flooding visitors' browsers with popups, alerts and sign-up forms. It's the worst experience possible on the web and does absolutely nothing to build credibility with those you want to connect with.

Building trust with storytelling

How can you win the battle to get someone's attention? Storytelling. But not just any story; it has to be a story where the reader becomes the central character. If you understand the needs of your audience and what they're looking for to make their lives easier, they will recognise themselves in the plot. They'll identify with the challenges preventing them from achieving their goal, and crucially, they'll recognise how your product or service will be of value to them.

People love a good story. They're easy for us to understand because there's context and a logical sequence of events to help us make sense of them. The best stories are those with unexpected drama or adversity overcome by a successful solution.

Think of the characters in your favourite movie, or even people on reality TV shows. We get to know their personalities, see their battle scars and accept their vulnerabilities, willing them on as they grow in strength and confidence to cross the finish line. Stories define us as human beings.

Everyone has stories about how they found a need for a product, how they were forced to look for a way to adapt to or survive a difficult experience, or how inside knowledge gave them a unique perspective. Stories help people to bond and form a connection, and that's what makes them so powerful in business communications.

Businesses have stories, too, but unless you're in a market for commodity products, people buy from people. We're all far more ready to learn from and be inspired by the stories of people we feel a connection with. You can see this simply by looking at the number of Twitter followers prominent entrepreneurs have compared to their businesses. At the time of writing, Tesla has 3.5m followers on Twitter, while founder Elon Musk has a following of 40m. Microsoft founder Bill Gates has amassed a staggering 52m followers compared to his former company's 9m. Richard Branson has 12m followers compared to the Virgin Group's 250,000. These are the people who make the stories, create intrigue and court controversy, but ultimately, they influence and endear us towards what makes them who they are.

Stories build brands. They have more value and interest than many people give them credit for, so use them to your advantage, build connections and invest in these relationships to reward people's trust.

Tone of voice

The tone of your content is incredibly important if it's to reflect the brand you're building. The way you speak (and this applies to the written just as much as the spoken word) shouldn't be contrived. For many companies, it can present an opportunity to be different or stand out in the marketplace.

We're all familiar with the concept of brand guidelines, but there's an increasing number of company leaders publishing their own content guidelines. These are the people who show a deep understanding not only of digital channels, but also their audience, as well as their purpose and what they're striving to achieve.

One of my favourite examples comes from 'challenger bank' Monzo. Banking has for decades been dominated by long-established traditional organisations that over recent years have lost the respect of most of their customers. Research published by global management consulting firm Bain & Company in 2018 found that 54% of respondents would trust a big technology company with their money more than their bank, and only 41% of people would recommend their primary bank to their friends.[39] As deregulation of the banking sector has gathered pace in the UK, technology companies have capitalised on the opportunities this presents, not only through new products and services, but also in the way they speak about them.

Monzo is among an increasing number of companies, including Ikea and Airbnb, publishing its own tone of voice guidelines. These companies' leaders recognise the competitiveness of their space and push the experience of being a customer with them as a positive differentiator against their competitors. The Virgin brand is another great example of a business that has a huge personality, which is reflected in just about all of its communication.

When thinking about your own content, consider what's important to you and what will resonate with your audience. Is yours a fun, spirited business like many modern start-ups, or does the nature of your industry demand a more muted and professional tone for you to be taken seriously? Are you speaking to a niche or even exclusive audience that appreciates your language and style, or are you appealing to a mass-market? Do you throw caution to the wind and be bold, even experimental, with your content? Or is it important to be seen as a safe pair of hands?

---

39 'In search of customers who love their bank', Bain & Company, 2018, www.bain.com/contentassets/7c3b1535c4444f7b8a078c577078a705/bain_report-in_search_of_customers_who_love_their_bank-2018.pdf

Creating a content strategy

Having a set of content standards in place ensures consistent communication across all your different channels and acknowledges the attributes of the audiences you're communicating with, but this can only happen once you've defined who they are from the 'Audience' step in the DISTANCE process. After you've considered the tone of voice for your content, the next step is to determine how you'll plan and manage it. This is known as a content strategy.

Planning a content strategy is a process in itself that wouldn't normally include the creation of content. Instead, it includes researching the style and format of the content you require, planning core messaging priorities, identifying how you'll create and deliver content, and how it will be measured and reported on.

Many websites, especially corporate websites, suffer from content bloat. It might be that as new products were launched, microsites were built to accompany them, or team profiles may have been added but not removed, or pages that once seemed a good idea have never gained any traction with visitors. A survey by the World Bank on its own content found that over 31% of its policy reports were never downloaded.[40]

---

40 'Which World Bank reports are widely read?', The World Bank, no date, https://documents.worldbank.org/en/publication/documents-reports/documentdetail/387501468322733597/which-world-bank-reports-are-widely-read

Imagine what else could have been done with the time people spent creating those reports!

The content strategy process for a new website project begins with an audit: a detailed look at the existing content to identify how relevant it is for now and the future. If you're copying existing content into a new website (only ever after an audit), the more content you opt to keep, the more work you'll need to do to ensure any external links to it are not broken.

Many people wrongly assume that getting rid of content will harm search engine rankings. In reality, if no one is visiting (or linking to) your content, no one will be missing out when you get rid of it. Keeping old or outdated pages simply makes it harder to manage content in the future and risks content sprawl. Unchecked, this can add unnecessary costs in terms of file storage and backup, as well as presenting a confusing structure and inaccurate off-brand messaging.

Reviewing your website analytics will show you which pages are the most popular and speaking to your customers will give you valuable insight into what drew them towards these pages and why. Are people finding you for the first time through these pages? Or are they attracting existing customers? What stage in the journey are these customers at? Are they making comparisons or just about to buy from you?

Your content strategy also covers your approach to distributing and repurposing content. High-quality content takes valuable time and resource to produce, so just because you've published it, don't assume your job is done when it's 'out there'. Make quality over quantity your motto. There's no harm in referring back to older content or publishing it multiple times in several places. Your strategy should dictate where and when you'll republish content and with what frequency, so you can achieve maximum cut through with your audience and return from your investment in creating it.

Connecting content

Building your content strategy will identify the process and purpose for creating your content. But your content also needs to be structured in a way that it becomes manageable for your team, and both helpful and discoverable for your audience. As audiences consume content across an ever more proliferated range of devices and systems become increasingly connected, so too must your content. The rules and structures put in place to manage this content is known as information architecture (IA).

Companies produce vast quantities of content so the strength of your IA will be measured by how easily people can find what matters to them. IA determines how different elements of your content might relate to each other, how they could be grouped and how they might be found through search or menu features.

To illustrate the point, think of a museum that has a vast collection of artifacts – not all of which might be on display at the same time. In addition to each item having a description, it will be catalogued to allow researchers to quickly identify when and where an object was found, how it relates to other items in the collection and where it might be displayed. The level of detail could be extended to include references to the archaeological team who made the discovery and incorporate their wider experience or specific areas of interest to support future work.

To relate this to your website, every time you see the heading, 'You might also be interested in', you're seeing the results of IA. Large news sites such as the BBC are able to report on a story and include links to other stories that might be related by geography, topic or specific individuals.

Publishing a blog post in isolation will likely see visitors click on and off the page through a single-entry point, such as a search result. By relating that post to other relevant content, both you and your audience stand to gain value from it as people spend more time on your site and find further relevant content to support their goal.

It's worth pointing out that IA is not the same as planning your navigation. Much of it sits behind the scenes, but how you group your content will inform and influence how you direct others to find it which has a wider influence on the overall visitor experience.

Creating content assets

Over the years, I've spoken to lots of business leaders who say they struggle to find content worth sharing. What they really mean is they've not paused to give thought to the type of content that would be valuable to their audience.

With a smartphone in their pocket, everyone has the potential to be a photographer, videographer and podcaster, so everyone can create content quickly and easily. I would absolutely advocate that you use this content to your advantage. Videos you make yourself might not feel very professional, but they naturally tend to have more personality and can be more endearing to viewers than a professional shoot. People love to see you for who you are, rather than wonder whether they're seeing a misrepresentation or even being misled. It adds to the all-important authenticity.

That said, the value of a strong set of core content assets will be immediately noticeable to visitors coming to your site. Self-made videos are ideal for LinkedIn and images snapped on your phone can help you to get your message across, but professionally lit, framed and edited visual content will help you to build a library of assets that you'll refer back to over and over again.

Most business leaders find the same conversations coming up time and time again. This is your written content opportunity. If you feel short of ideas for content, then think about all the questions your customers ask during the pre- or post-sales conversations, the reasons they buy from you and pain points solved by your product or service. Imagine what a tour of your business would look like. What would you show people and tell them? Testimonials and award wins can add an element of 'social proof' that validates and supports your broader content and, of course, contributes to raising your profile as well.

If you're afraid of repeating content that others might have already shared, then find a different perspective, add your own opinions or relate it to your personal experience. While there might be dozens of similar articles out there, they don't have your name on them; their creators don't share your audience, so never assume that people have seen the content elsewhere, or they know about the expertise you're valued for. Plus, wouldn't you prefer it that your audience found your content rather than someone else's?

This is why content is so critical to modern marketing. We're all only a Google search away from finding it, and the more your content resonates with your audience, the more likely you'll see results from it.

Copywriting for the web

Writing good copy for your website is a skill that ensures your message is clearly and concisely communicated while condensing the word count. Interestingly, the Nielsen study referenced earlier in the chapter also found that 'promotional language imposes a cognitive burden on users who have to spend resources on filtering out the hyperbole to get at the facts'. In the age where just about anything can be labelled as 'fake news', people are generally less trusting of advertising and more likely to be discouraged by overly promotional language. With widespread reviews and social media opinion only a few clicks away, any over-confidence in your own writing can quickly come undone.

Let's have a look at the key ingredients for good content, and what doesn't work so well.

Headlines

Headlines have existed since the dawn of the printing press. To this day, they are every bit as important to attract attention and engage your readers.

When you're writing on the web, headlines serve two main purposes:

1. They grab your reader's attention as they scan your page

2. They support your search engine rankings

The importance of a good headline cannot be understated – ask any newspaper editor and they'll tell you the impact it can have on their daily sales. It is essential to attracting attention. While click-baity headlines might achieve engagement and make your social analytics look more favourable, great content will add value to your viewers and nurture a level of trust between you and them.

With people having diminishing attention spans, being clear about your message is vital if your website is going to capture visitors' attention. It takes about 50 milliseconds (that's 0.05 seconds) for users to form an opinion about your website that determines whether they'll stay or leave.[41] As you've done the hard work of attracting them to your site, it would seem a shame for them to simply walk back out the door because what they see doesn't encourage them to stay.

---

41   G Lindgaard et al, 'Attention web designers: You have 50 milliseconds to make a good first impression', *Behaviour & Information Technology*, March–April 2006, 25:2, 115–126

Stock photography

Stock photography has often been used on websites in the absence of professional images, but these photos can become immediately identifiable if they're not chosen carefully.

I understand that getting good photography in some industries can be challenging, if not bordering on impossible. Healthcare is a prime example, or where children might be involved. If you're having to use stock photography, make sure you look for images that represent the demographics of your customers, your region and a degree of 'real life'. I'd always recommend avoiding heavily stylised images of glass whiteboards or word clouds. They might pass for your internal PowerPoint presentation, but they won't cut it on your website.

Stock photography doesn't just need to come from sites selling stock images. Build up your own library of stock photography from activities taking place in your business. Keep photos of your people, workspace, process and products up to date for both your website and wider promotional activities. You'll be grateful for this stock of images the day you have an opportunity to appear in a press release or business publication, and in the meantime, good images can supplement your content for blog posts and social media.

PDF documents

A PDF file, essentially an on-screen version of a printed document, is commonly used for downloads from your website. Certain documents like brochures are almost impossible to replicate on your website, so it makes sense for the viewer to read them in the format they were originally intended for.

PDF documents are generally hard to view online and don't always make for a great experience. While search engines can index PDF files, why make it harder for people to find your content? Make presenting content within your website in the native HTML format your first priority, with PDFs only used for exceptions where the visual style of the content can't be easily replicated online. Although you can track clicks on to PDF files, you can't easily track other interactions, so another reason for adding your content directly to your website is so that you can measure visitor behaviour with tools like Google Analytics.

From a website management point of view, PDF documents are generally hard to maintain, so they're more likely to age on your website. Having to update the original document, recreate it as a PDF and upload it to the website all adds time to the process. Always remember how important your content is and how presenting it in the wrong format could lead to a lack of engagement or confusion as people try to access it.

If you really must have website content available as a PDF, my suggestion would be to publish it as a web page, but enable the on-demand creation of a PDF based on the same content. This reduces the risk of inaccurate or outdated content and gives the viewer the choice of their preferred format. I'll be willing to bet the web version will win every time.

Video

Every website should be capitalising on video. There are various different formats that might be suitable depending on your brand style, sector and budget. These typically include:

- Vlogs (these are more suited to social media in my view)

- Interviews

- Tutorials

- Product overviews

- Presentations or speaking events

- Testimonials

- Webinar recordings

Research from Wyzowl suggests that 81% of marketers say video has helped increase the average time their visitors spend on a page, with a massive 95% saying video has helped increase user understanding of their product or service.[42] Crucially, though, video adds personality to your business, so not only is it more convenient for visitors to engage with, you can also tell your story in a compelling way to encourage the next steps you want them to take.

Video is easy to create these days. Most people have a film and production studio in their pockets with the capabilities now found in smartphones. While it may sound counterintuitive, not all videos need to be studio-based and professionally produced. As people are invariably looking for connection, personal videos with a more amateurish feel can actually make a stronger impact, depending on where they're posted.

My advice would be to use home-made videos on your personal profile or social media channels, where people are more likely to follow people. There's also an expectation that social content can be more throwaway – here today, gone tomorrow (unless, of course, it goes viral). Website videos, on the other hand, will likely need more planning and staging, be that for a formal presentation, explaining a concept, showcasing product features or a fun, quirky introduction.

You'll probably have noticed how video is increasingly appearing in Google's search results, too, so having a presence on YouTube is valuable from a

---

42   Wyzowl, 'Video marketing statistics 2021', 2021, www.wyzowl.com/
video-marketing-statistics-2020

reach and visibility perspective, as well as providing another channel for people to follow you.

Podcasts

Podcasting is nothing new. It's been around for over ten years, but has seen a relatively sudden meteoric rise with huge investments in content that have mirrored the growth seen by popular TV streaming services like Amazon Prime, Netflix and Disney Plus. Spotify has invested hundreds of millions of dollars in audio content, Amazon has recently acquired podcasting network Wondery, and Twitter has bought podcasting app Breaker in a multimillion dollar deal. Forbes is predicting podcasting as the new battleground for big tech,[43] which matters because a precedent has been set by the growth of other media and social media channels before.

The growth in podcasting presents increased commercial opportunities to create your own content, build relationships and raise your profile. Podcast listeners in the UK alone reached over 15m in 2020, with forecasts predicting close to 20m listeners by 2024.[44] Further research by the BBC found that brand mentions in podcasts deliver on average 16% higher

---

43 J Koetsier, 'Podcasting is the new battleground for big tech as Twitter buys Breaker', *Forbes*, 2021, www.forbes.com/sites/johnkoetsier/2021/01/04/podcasting-is-the-new-battleground-for-big-tech-as-twitter-buys-breaker
44 Statista Research Department, 'Podcasts in the UK – statistics & facts', statista.com, 2020, www.statista.com/topics/6908/podcasts-in-the-uk

engagement and 12% higher memory encoding than the surrounding content. The research also found the more intimate and conversational podcasts created an elevated state of engagement for brand mentions, helping to generate lifts in awareness by 89%, brand consideration by 57%, brand favourability by 24% and purchase intent by 14%.[45]

Recording a podcast can be as simple as using the voice recorder on your smartphone to create an audio file that can then be uploaded to a podcast hosting service for distribution across popular podcast listening apps. As your podcast audience grows, you may consider more advanced production that ultimately leads to direct monetisation of your content through sponsored episodes, premium content or offline events that sit alongside your existing products and services. Many podcasts are now also broadcast on YouTube or shared as live events, providing a great opportunity to broaden your own network of contacts and reach new audiences.

Podcasts have longevity and a back catalogue of episodes can be hugely valuable for sharing your personality and extending your reach across different platforms. With such large investments taking place in the industry, it will be interesting to see how Google

---

45 BBC Media Centre, 'Audio:Activated – New BBC Global News study reveals unique effectiveness of branded podcasts', BBC, 2019, www. bbc.co.uk/mediacentre/worldnews/2019/audio-activated

will approach the indexing of audio content alongside existing searches in the years to come.

Content first

The irony of 'content first' in this book is that it falls at the end of the chapter! Now you know the scope of content, why should your content come first?

As you're planning your website, I implore you to take a content-first approach. Your content will be an integral part of your design, so knowing what format it's going to be in, how long it might be and what tone it will take is crucial to the UX. Your content will also influence how the site is structured (known as the IA) so visitors can easily find the information they're looking for.

I'm not suggesting you need to know every aspect of your content and have it ready word-for-word, but the more you do know about your content, the more you can plan its creation and make provision for it during the technical stages of the website build. This will smooth the process of publishing, promoting and maintaining it.

One of the challenges many people have with content first is visualising it on their website. If you take this out of the equation and think in terms of what you want visitors to take away from your site, the visual elements don't matter at this stage.

Many people also assume that they can work on the content while the website is being built, but this invariably results in it not being ready for when it's time to add it to the website. Populating the site takes time and you'll likely want to shuffle elements around as you're adding them, so it's not as straightforward as simply copy and paste. Failing to appreciate and prepare the content needed for the site is one of the main reasons projects miss their deadline. It's easily underestimated and too important to risk leaving it to the end.

Summary

The content on your website is one of the most fundamental aspects of your planning process. Why would you want a website with no content? Your visitors are looking for answers, and your content allows them to move to the next stage of doing business with you.

Content is basically everything within your website. Whatever content you're planning for your site, it all needs to link together to give a clear and consistent message, build trust and drive the actions you want your visitors to take.

Great content establishes your authority, but how can you achieve this if people aren't reading it? The answer comes with the use of storytelling where the visitor is the lead character. If you understand their needs and what they're looking for, they will recognise themselves in the story and be more inclined to take action.

The content strategy process for a new website project begins with a content audit: a detailed look at the existing content to identify how relevant it is. If you'll be copying existing content into a new website after your audit, you will need to ensure any external links to it are not broken. If you feel short of ideas for content, think about all the questions your customers ask, the reasons people buy from you and the pain points your product or service has solved.

Actions

Using your learnings from this chapter, create a content plan for the next three to six months. This will be a baseline covering key themes in your business or market that you can expand on across different channels.

Review your current website content (ie perform a content audit) to identify the most popular pages or blog posts. How can you provide more useful content? Could you make this easier to find by deleting older content that is less popular? What are the common questions your audience asks about your products and services that can inspire new content opportunities?

What are the questions your audience asks you? What is the language they use? Can you dispel myths, explain jargon or technical terms, or answer common questions that keep cropping up?

Complete an audience problem statement in the format of 'I am a [person] who is trying to [achieve a goal] but [barrier in the way] because [I have a problem] which makes me feel [emotional state]'. Avoid putting the solution in the problem statement, but focus on the problem people come to you for help with.

By extension of your problem statement, use a technique such as a mind map that shows different branches to explore subtopics, helping you to build up a variety of content themes around a core topic or statement.

Review your social media output. How often are you re-using your content? How much of it has been repurposed to other channels (note: repurposing content is not simply publishing the same words and pictures across all your social media, but adjusting and optimising for your respective audiences)?

10
Execution

'Our goals can only be reached through a vehicle of a plan. There is no other route to success.'
—Pablo Picasso

With the first seven steps in the DISTANCE method now complete, you should have a sense of how you want to approach your new website and be in a position to start pulling together information to develop a more detailed brief and technical requirement. You'll probably have a pretty good idea of the scale of the site you're wanting to build and how it will fit in with other elements of your business and wider strategy. In this chapter, we'll cover how you can identify who needs to be part of your project, including choosing an agency partner, and setting the project scope and timeframe for delivery.

There's a common yet mistaken belief with websites that the sooner the project is started, the sooner it will be finished. Debunking this myth is essentially the purpose of this book! In fact, websites shouldn't really be classed as 'projects'. The build stage might have a defined start and end point, but beyond that, digital is never done. It's once the site launches that the hard work really begins. We'll cover more on that in the final chapter.

Having considered all the various attributes of your website and what it will do for you, you need at this stage to decide how you'll go about the design and technical development to bring it to life. Larger companies may have the option of an in-house team, or you may choose to work with a specialist agency like A Digital. Alternatively, freelancers can be an effective choice for short-term projects or where more specialist knowledge is required.

	Pros	Cons
Agency	Specialist advice, often from a multidisciplinary background with an established team. Cross-sector experience (or specialist sector knowledge). An external perspective on cultural norms in your business or industry. Agencies often have access to specialist tools and software that may be costly or difficult to justify for freelances or in-house teams.	Higher cost both in terms of build and ongoing maintenance. Building a relationship and mutual understanding is an investment in itself and specific industry knowledge may be lacking. Agencies have other clients and aim to maximise capacity.
Freelance	Greater flexibility to choose your own team of professionals. Typically available at a lower cost than hiring an agency. Require less commitment than hiring an agency or recruiting your own in-house team. Often flexibility with schedules and timeframes.	Provision of ongoing support can be limited as freelancers tend to move from project-to-project. Single individuals can become a performance bottleneck. Freelancers tend to specialise in a given skill rather than offering a multidisciplinary experience.

Continued

Cont.

	Pros	Cons
In-house	The greatest level of flexibility – your team will always be working for you on your own projects.	You need to have a clear roadmap for growth to keep your team busy with ongoing tasks.
	The team will be closest to your market and products, as well as internal communications.	Appropriate leadership and continual learning and development required to keep skills up to date.
	Agility to switch between priorities.	It requires multiple disciplines to create a strong in-house team.
	Increased transparency and control over production/delivery.	Recruitment and retention needs a lot of attention.
		There can be a temptation for scope creep as a team's remit covers a wider range of digital tasks than it did originally (often to save costs or keep teams busy).

Working with an agency partner

By now, you should have a view on the type of digital partnership you'll need. If you choose to work with an agency partner, you'll find there are several different types with some being more suitable for your brief than others.

Full-service agencies typically offer services across brand, creative and digital, and provide most services a business will need under one roof. In truth, though, only the largest of agencies can honestly claim to be 'full-service' without contracting in more specialist support. Full-service agencies may be able to provide the breadth of creative and strategic guidance you need, but not always the depth of digital experience.

Specialist *digital agencies* have a focus on digital coupled with the knowledge of what works best online and the appropriate mix of skills to deliver it. Finally, *niche* or *boutique agencies* might limit themselves to particular sectors, or even specific aspects of digital tactics such as conversion rate optimisation or building sales funnels.

Whichever type of agency you choose (and there may be times when you need more than one), it's important to realise that building a website and delivering successful campaigns is a collaborative effort. While you can leave elements of technical work to others, it's vital to invest the time in building a strong and transparent relationship so everyone is aware of who's responsible for what. It takes time to find and hire an agency, so making a long-term commitment to working together that both sides can see value in will naturally lead to stronger results.

Choosing an agency partner

If you're serious about building a successful agency partnership, then simply sending a brief or invitation to tender to all the agencies you can find on the first page of Google isn't going to get you off to the best start. There is so much that is flawed with tender and selection processes for digital projects, which is another reason for this book. Arming people with the right knowledge for commissioning websites is key for them to make sensible choices for their project and ambitions.

Even with the knowledge shared within this book, you should still expect an agency partner you approach to help you shape your brief. This might form part of their response to your enquiry, or you might even choose to engage them in a 'mini' discovery project that stands apart from a full website build. This would give you the chance to trial working together on a commercial basis and help you to narrow down your project scope within the framework the DISTANCE method provides.

A good agency partner will interrogate your brief and give you the opportunity to challenge them in return. If agencies ask for your plans for growth, then it's reasonable that you as a client can expect to know theirs. This question doesn't only help to answer your brief, but helps both parties understand what the longer-term prospects for the relationship might be.

Ultimately, if your growth ambitions or wider world-views aren't a close match, the relationship can sour sooner rather than later, and you find yourself back at square one. If this happens after you've made technology or strategic decisions based on the advice of the agency you've chosen, it clearly places a limitation on how you can move forwards with a replacement. Being clear about what you want to see from your agency partner in addition to 'a new website' is important to ensure working together is fun and meets your respective expectations.

One thing never to ask an agency partner for is design work up front or 'on spec' as part of your selection process. There are plenty of other more effective ways to evaluate agencies; turning the process into a beauty parade while expecting them to meet unknown expectations wastes valuable effort and fails to establish the firm foundation required for a long-term relationship.

Engaging with stakeholders

The entire premise of the Go the DISTANCE process is to step back and consider the bigger picture within which your website must reside. This means you'll need to engage with stakeholders from across the business who can have their voice heard and give the project their support. Successful websites need inputs from a variety of people (and perhaps entire departments), so it's essential to ensure that each member of the team understands the broader business strategy, why the project is important to the organisation and the new opportunities it will provide.

While stakeholder engagement is essential, you don't necessarily want all of them to be directly involved with every stage of the project. Bringing too many people into the project can result in 'design by committee' where everyone has an opinion (usually based on their own personal rather than professional experience), which can lead to slow decision making and introduce an unhelpful battle of political wills. When this happens, there's a real risk that those involved design a site for themselves, losing focus on the real reasons for embarking on the project and those who will ultimately be using it. Can you imagine a focus group for the first Apple iPhone being told there would be no keyboard?

On the flipside, not including the right stakeholders runs the risk of crucial input arriving late in the project, derailing progress or unexpectedly widening the scope. American usability author and researcher Jared Spool calls this an 'executive swoop and poop', likening it to a seagull that swoops into a project, poops all over the work done so far and flies off, leaving someone else to clean up the mess.[46]

Stakeholders who are involved need to share ownership in the work being produced. This gives them the strength and confidence to present work to their internal colleagues and visibility of any agency partner's work behind the scenes. Stakeholder involvement is also an opportunity for an agency partner to share their knowledge with your team members, set-

---

46 JM Spool, 'Preventing the executive swoop and poop with design sprints', Medium, 2016, https://jmspool.medium.com/preventing-the-executive-swoop-and-poop-with-design-sprints-c01545490f76

ting a standard for what 'good' should look like while preparing them for the activities that lie ahead once the site launches.

As an agency owner, I often find myself being approached by prospective clients because they don't feel they're getting the level of services they should be from their existing agency, or they struggle to see the value in what they're paying for. While relationships do run their natural course, building alignment and having the right people around the table ensures trust and confidence to achieve the best results.

Setting a timescale

If there's one certainty with any digital project, it's that there's no end. I make no apology for repeating this point because I've seen so many websites fall into disrepair through a lack of upkeep, the perception being that only a full replacement can fix it. It becomes a boom-and-bust cycle with each revision carrying the promise of doing things differently, but old habits die hard.

That being said, when you're building a website, there has to be a point at which to launch it.

Deadlines

Timescales are vital in business and fundamental to goal setting. Deadlines bring order and focus to our busy lives, allowing us to confidently 'tick the box' and move on to the next item on our task list. But while deadlines can help to guard against scope creep (a project manager's nemesis) and reduce the risk of project fatigue, they can also be damaging to digital projects.

Like goals, deadlines need to be sensible and realistic. An arbitrary deadline without a clear rationale can end up with a sprint to the finish line, resulting in poor-quality code, incomplete testing or compromises on performance. Unrealistically short or inflexible deadlines will deter the best agency partners and developers, not only because of the added time pressure, but because time-based deadlines shift the delivery to a calendar date, rather than the needs of users.

Of course, there are perfectly valid deadlines, such as coordinated campaign launches, seasonal buying habits or events. These may ultimately be time-based, but a focus on the reason for the deadline allows functionality and features to be prioritised based on what users will expect or the actions they need to take.

Poorly planned projects that don't focus on your audience are almost certain to miss their deadline, so it's preferable to slow things down early on in the planning process to ensure there's complete clarity of what is being built for when. Releasing a half-baked website for the sake of hitting a deadline can do tremendous damage to your brand and be immensely disheartening for your team.

Software development by its very nature will demand a period of testing and bug fixing, with more complex projects requiring more time allocated to this. Bugs are inevitable in any software, and the time it takes to fix them can sometimes be an unknown quantity.

It's worth adding that deadlines work both ways and are as important for your development partner as they are for you if you're going to keep to time. Certain phases of development carry prerequisites that can fall beyond your web team's remit, and failing to provide these on time can quickly disrupt the schedule and momentum with your project.

Building a broad roadmap with a series of logically ordered high-level milestones based on months or even quarters can help to put a shape on a project, especially where delivery is likely to be spread over a longer period of time or involve a series of phased releases.

Creating a specification

Historically, there's been an expectation that software projects should be accompanied by lengthy specification documents that allow you to definitively sign off each individual feature, but specifications generally don't account for what your audience needs to do and what they experience. A requirement that states 'customers can pay online' is too vague and overlooks critical elements of the process at this stage of the visitor journey.

That said, specifying features in minute detail isn't a good use of time because things can change and the specification can quickly become out of date, requiring amendment for it to be useful. The time taken in preparing detailed specifications is better spent implementing features around more broad guidelines and testing them to ensure they meets user needs.

The approach my agency takes is based on the creation of a site map. Site maps themselves have their own pros and cons, but with an outline of the pages in front of us, my team and I can consider three things for each section or page:

- What will visitors *see*?

- What types of content will be needed on this page?

- What should visitors be able to *do*?

These elements are a convenient extension of the empathy mapping we looked at in Chapter 7 as we considered audience and actions. They're also easily built upon as you learn more about your audience over time, drawing on the principal of a minimal

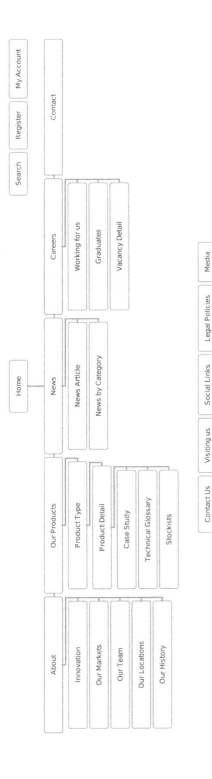

A simplified extract from a site map that sets the basis for a flexible specification

viable product (MVP) which was popularised in the book *The Lean Startup* by Eric Ries.[47]

When you're working towards an MVP, rather than pouring huge energy into creating the perfect website based on a detailed specification, focus on the minimum requirements to launch, enabling you to gather feedback from your audience. In other words, a usable website that meets your core audience requirements allows faster progress than aspiring to go live with an absolutely perfect site (which, as I'm sure you know by now, doesn't exist). This level of specification offers guidance while leaving room for design or logical interpretation based on user feedback, lessons learned or new data that comes to light.

There will be times when more detailed process flows or schematics may be required, particularly to define complex functionality. These diagrams might indicate interactions with other systems, triggers for email notifications or specific processes that may be dependent on a number of different conditions, but they are more reflective of process mapping than a detailed specification. Your development partner needs to be allowed to use their professional experience to define the finer details of what the site will deliver based on established best practice and the available

---

47   E Ries, *The Lean Startup: How constant innovation creates radically successful businesses* (Portfolio Penguin, 2011)

data. A rigid specification document can soon become outdated, taking up yet more project time to revise and review the content.

Taking an MVP approach will typically result in building prototypes that leave you with options for how far you choose to develop features and functionality against the backdrop of expected returns or value added to the UX. Creating a base level of functionality is less likely to demand costly wholesale changes and allows your decisions to be informed by data, rather than gut feel.

The difference between a typical product or website strategy (top) and an MVP approach (bottom). Adapted from an original image by Henrik Kniberg.[48]

---

48   This image has been adapted from an original by Henrik Kniberg (https://blog.crisp.se/2016/01/25/henrikkniberg/making-sense-of-mvp)

Design sprints

The MVP approach has been further refined into the concept of design 'sprints', popularised in the book of the same name written by Jake Knapp during his time at Google Ventures.[49] He defines a design sprint as a five-day process for answering critical business questions through design, prototyping and testing ideas with customers. Google Ventures calls the approach a 'greatest hits' of business strategy, innovation, behavioural science and design thinking. I wouldn't advocate this approach for your entire website, but the method can be incredibly powerful when you're planning specific features or launching new products.

The design sprint approach has been widely adopted by companies including Slack and Airbnb, the entire focus being on validating design ideas with as little effort as possible. Only those that can be validated are developed, allowing resource to be directed towards delivering the most valuable returns.

Project management

How your project is delivered will largely be down to who you decide to have on your team. An agency partner will likely have their own approach, while freelancers might work to a fixed time-based term in a

---

49 J Knapp *Sprint: How to solve big problems and test new ideas in just five days*, Simon Schuster, 2016

more ad hoc way. If you have your own internal team, it will be crucial to formulate a clear approach to managing both the build and ongoing development, no doubt among other projects.

There are two widely accepted approaches to delivering website projects: waterfall and agile. Each approach has its pros and cons, with agile having been developed in response to some of the constraints presented by its predecessor, waterfall.

Waterfall projects are the simplest type and take their name from the way they appear on project plans or Gantt charts (bar charts, named after their inventor Henry Gantt, that show a project schedule). Tasks are listed and generally completed one after the other in a specific order from start to finish, one step at a time. Following the tasks in this order makes for a linear approach with a clear path to completion and milestones and deadlines along the way.

Agile is an iterative approach with shorter incremental steps to achieving a goal, releasing ongoing benefits rather than them only being realised at the end of a project. Agile projects follow a much looser approach with goals focused on delivering on a user requirement (technically known as a user story), rather than working to an organised timeline. Each phase of development, known as a sprint, will run for a fixed period of time, with tasks drawn from a backlog of prioritised deliverables. Any items from the backlog that aren't completed may be pushed into subsequent sprints.

The agile approach is generally favoured for large, complex projects that need to be refined over time. Digital products will generally fall into this category, and this approach is closely related to design thinking and the MVP principal we've already covered.

Waterfall projects, by comparison, can help you to achieve your goals with greater clarity and ordered progression. The problem with waterfall projects is the order is quickly lost if the end goal changes, impacting on the overall plan. With this approach, you're basically taking aim at a goal and hoping the target doesn't move. As we've seen in web projects, new information often comes to light as you progress, so aiming for a fixed target can create the same problem as a detailed specification: the project becomes too rigid and there's no room for movement to improve on the desired outcome.

The nature of waterfall projects can also limit collaboration as this more traditional approach can result in people working within their own silos. Designers work with other designers through the design phase, passing the project on to developers to handle the next stage. Developers then pass their work on to testers and so on. Without clear communication between each team, the reasons why something has been done the way it has can be missed, resulting in poor decisions being taken or a lack of understanding of the challenges that might face the current direction. This can lead to a 'big reveal' to clients as work reaches the end of the chain, which more likely than not turns into a 'big disappointment' as a lack of collaboration weakens the end result.

Waterfall projects, having a fixed critical path and usually a defined timescale, tend to be easier to budget for than agile ones. Time basically determines when something is done. Agile, being an iterative approach, doesn't share the same view on 'done'. Done is when the user story has been satisfied, and budgeting for costs can be based on a number of pre-determined sprints. With agile sprints including a review period (known as a retrospective), it's always possible to learn and improve on a story and its outcome, so allowing for additional sprints will require some leeway with your budget.

A hybrid approach

While there are purists out there who will argue that a project should take one form or another, it is possible to combine more traditional approaches with agile methods. In my view, this offers the best of both worlds, and can work particularly well for build projects where certain milestones need to be achieved before you can move into a phase of iterative and ongoing development that plays well into agile methods.

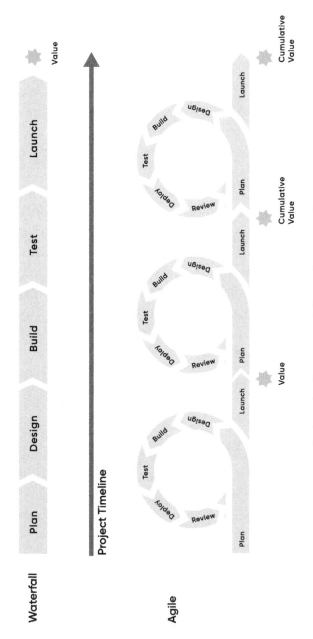

Project timelines, waterfall vs agile approaches

For most website projects, a hybrid approach can strike a balance between effective collaboration and allowing your development team or agency to lead based on their experience. The combined approach will generally borrow several principals from agile, combining them with a more traditional task-based approach.

The particular benefits of incorporating agile practices into the initial build are:

- User stories that focus on audience requirements

- A collaborative approach

- Incremental and iterative development

- Working in sprints with daily stand-up meetings

- Ongoing testing

- Smaller and quicker releases

Combining these with the more traditional waterfall approach, you can still maintain:

- Time-bound deadlines

- Concurrent tasks (such as content creation while development is in progress)

- Predictable phases of work

Whether you choose an agile, waterfall or hybrid method, the naming of your approach and how rigorously you stick to certain practices within it isn't important. What matters is to find a rhythm that works for you and your chosen team that retains the flexibility to draw on a range of individual experiences and learnings from previous projects, be they website related or not.

As a minimum, you need a framework in place so you can organise resources and progress towards your goal. I would advocate the iterative approach every day of the week, but exactly how your project is managed will come down to the capabilities in your team and your own digital culture. Knowing the benefits and drawbacks of each approach will allow you to see how you can break down your project into manageable packages of work, support budgeting and, of course, plan other activities and campaigns off the back of it.

Giving feedback

Being critical of someone's work can be an awkward point in a project, yet for collaboration to be effective, there has to be a feedback loop. But what makes good, constructive feedback that upholds the goals of your project?

Focus on the objective. Consider whether your feedback will impact on your overall goal. Making your logo more prominent or enlarging social media icons is unlikely to impact on the number of leads your site can generate.

Review from your audience's perspective. We all have personal opinions, but it's vital to detach yourself from looking at your website through your own personal experience. You might not fall within the target market and your personal browsing habits may be unhelpful to the project. Let data provide insight and be prepared to test and refine as you go. Few things with your website should be set in stone, especially with modern CMSs providing extensive options for updating it without needing access to the codebase.

Avoid providing solutions. Constructive feedback should be a discussion. If you're determined to provide solutions, design and development teams risk becoming reactive rather than proactive. Have an open conversation that allows you to explore alternatives and avoids people losing confidence over their delivery.

Leave room for compromise. Achieving a desired outcome together with your teams and partners builds a mutually respectful understanding that deepens the trust and confidence in your working relationship.

Patience will save you time. There's always excitement about reviewing a new design or testing new functionality, but it makes sense to wait until you've been asked before providing feedback. Work in progress is likely to have bugs that, in most cases, developers will know about. Discussing these before developers have tested their work and shared their findings for feedback wastes time.

Summary

This chapter has provided some insight into how website projects are typically managed in ways that allow timely delivery while ensuring successful collaboration. Planning and preparation stands for nothing if the execution is poor and mistakes at this point can undermine all the hard work completed in the preceding steps of the DISTANCE method.

You should now be able to identify which elements of your website carry the highest priority and how you might break up the project into manageable chunks that fulfil the needs of your roadmap while working within the constraints of budget, time and scope.

Actions

Using your learnings from this chapter, consider how your website project can be broken down into key phases that allow for iterative development. Is there an MVP in what you're working towards?

What are the features you like in your current website? While a new website is an upgrade, you'll want to make sure the things you like about your current site are part of the upgrade (rather than removed) just as much as you want to see the things you don't like gone.

What might your long-term roadmap for your website or digital products and services look like? Might there be options for eCommerce? How could new features on your website enhance the experience your customers enjoy? Are there any events or product launches that are going to impact on a deadline for your website?

How might your execution plan impact other stages in the DISTANCE method, such as strategy or technology?

Build a shortlist of no more than three to five agency partners you can engage with for your project. Get a feel for how they operate and what sort of feedback they've had from other clients. Gather a series of questions to present to agencies as part of your selection process. What are the attributes you're looking for in an agency beyond their pricing?

PART THREE
GOING THE DISTANCE

'The business enterprise has two—and
only two—basic functions: marketing
and innovation.'
Peter Drucker

11

It's Time To Go The DISTANCE

'Excellent firms don't believe in excellence – only in constant improvement and constant change.'
   —Tom Peters

Fast forward a few months and your shiny new website has been launched with much acclaim and fanfare. Your team has worked incredibly hard to pull together the required content, review the site and plan a successful launch, but what comes next? How can you go forward to grow into a great digital business that befits the post-pandemic world we live in?

There are literally dozens of directions you can take with your website once it's live. Add in all the different aspects of your digital marketing that wrap around your site, and there could easily be several more chapters added to this book. But having been through the DISTANCE method, you've probably got a fair idea of which tactics you'll use and what you need to know about them. I never set out to explain all the different approaches to marketing your website, but to show the depth of planning needed to build a successful site that can be well supported to becoming a valuable asset that aids your organisation's digital transformation.

You've built your website with the foresight of a digital strategy so it can Go the DISTANCE. Your roadmap is laid out in front of you, but you need to make it all happen. The hard work starts now.

This final chapter isn't about choosing an ad platform, running A/B tests or how you optimise your organic SEO performance, although all those things are likely to be relevant and feature in your tactics to deliver your strategy. This chapter is a summary of how you adapt your thinking, empower your team and innovate to ensure not only your site Goes the DISTANCE, but your business does, too.

Build your digital culture

Of course, not everyone will have been involved in the design of your website, so now is a good time to encourage more people from across your business to be interested in its outcomes. You've built a new asset, and now you need to get the most you can from it and the other assets you have, as well as continuing to invest in them for the future.

It's likely there'll be plenty of knowledge and expertise within your business. Sometimes, we get so close to what we do on a day-to-day basis, it's easy to think it's all common knowledge. But that's invariably not the case, so actively encourage people from across your business to engage with and contribute to your digital efforts. Get everyone listening out for cues from clients and customers, and even colleagues. Bottlenecks in processes, be they internal or external, need to be examined, questions people ask can be turned into awareness campaigns and the resulting valuable content should drive leads.

Like your website, your digital culture is something that needs regular nurturing. We're all creatures of habit, but it's vital you and your teams form new habits that will revolve around your customers and drive progress in your business. In most cases, your customers are already thinking digital first. They'll be checking your website, reading your reviews and looking you up on social media. If you have videos on YouTube, podcasts on Spotify and engage them with marketing automation, you'll stand out head and shoulders above competitors who are yet to embrace this digital-first approach to relationship building.

The key to remember with your digital culture is it's not about the technology. You may not have noticed as you read it, but the technology chapter is the shortest in this book! Technology is an enabler and facilitator, but it's only a small part of the overall process of becoming more digitally oriented; behaviours are driven by humans.

In larger organisations where you might have disparate teams, consider appointing someone who can unify their thinking, break down silos and remove the barriers that form a blockage to both the customer experience and your company's digital progress. This person (or team in the largest of companies) should facilitate open communication and information sharing, and even challenge departmental objectives with a view to refining them around digital thinking.

Invest in platforms and assets

The smart money these days is on media and assets. Every business has its own unique intellectual property (IP) that includes things like the founder's story, the company's achievements and innovations it's built along the way. But every company now also needs to be a media business, and the most successful companies are turning their IP into media assets such as video, podcasts or books. Those who scale to the next level are investing in platforms and software that allow their products and services to be delivered at scale across multiple locations through any device.

Take a look at companies like Uber and Airbnb. Uber disrupted the private hire transport market with clever yet simple technology, essentially providing transport as a service in the same way software was already being packaged. That same model has been extended into food delivery, freight and healthcare.

Airbnb used software to turn everyone's property into a rental home for holiday and business travellers. The company extended the accommodation capacity initially in major cities around the world, undercutting the prices advertised by hotels and booking providers like booking.com and laterooms.com. In time, its portfolio of quirky properties captured people's attention, and by introducing experiences with local guides and homeowners, Airbnb is now able to offer incomparably authentic and sharable travel adventures.

What's interesting with both Uber and Airbnb is they created their own digital assets. They had a clear purpose and scaled it with software. Uber doesn't own cars or employ drivers and Airbnb doesn't own property. Their software is able to match demand with supply and they broke the traditional mould, making it suddenly feel outdated.

What's so simple about both companies is they used software to solve existing human problems. Technology enables Uber to show you where the nearest car is. This solves the inconvenient problem of having to stand outside to hail a cab or hover on a taxi rank waiting for the next car to arrive. Airbnb gives homeowners with spare rooms a new income opportunity, while providing a cheaper alternative for guests who don't want to pay for an expensive hotel room at peak times.

These companies didn't set out to become overnight success stories. The way they innovated wasn't about becoming the next global disruptor; they happened to solve a problem that a lot of people have and technology has allowed them to scale globally.

You can look back and say what you have done was disruptive, but as we talked about in Chapter 5, make it your goal to be the best at what you do. It's about looking at your business and rethinking what it is you offer. Is British Airways an airline, or is it connecting communities and bringing people together? Was Kodak a camera company or did it enable people to make memories? Exploring questions like this for your own business can present new avenues to tackle the challenges in front of you, creating new products and services to solve people's problems that you can then scale.

Innovating in this way frees you from the traditional rules that might exist. Be bold and break the norm; be first. Throughout the pandemic, many companies were forced into thinking about how they needed to pivot to provide a new range of products and services to meet the sudden changes in the global environment. Those that reacted quickly may have found their true vocation. It may even have been more profitable than their original business. Time will tell how successful these pivots have been.

Empower people

It's key for people in an organisation with a strong digital culture to feel empowered to challenge the way things have always been done. They need to know they're actively encouraged to flag up new opportunities or share experiences they might have seen in their own personal digital habits that could pave the way for new platforms, products or customer experiences.

Digital presents a growing opportunity not only for companies, but also for individuals to get involved, learn new skills and bring their offline experience to develop online products. Rather than fear change or worry about their roles being taken over by automation, individuals can use this chance to spend more time looking at problems and identifying solutions as it presents fantastic opportunities for career growth.

While there are more products and services being delivered online, be cautious not to allow this to create distance between you and your customers or a culture that discourages personal contact. It's vital that online doesn't become a byword for 'remote' or 'distant', even though that's what it enables.

Online should mean being *more* connected, *more* convenient, real time and in the moment, while being available anywhere. Although I'm an advocate for using technology to automate tasks, it's important to avoid being seen as disconnected, unavailable or impersonal. Automation should allow you to spend *more* time speaking to your customers, listening and learning, helping you to shape future products and delivery. Use tools to become more accessible to people, as I'm still convinced that beyond a certain level, people buy from people. Allow technology to make things more efficient, but in a way that frees up people's time so they can make a greater impact in their work and purpose.

Many organisations will have seen cultural changes forced upon them through the global pandemic. The option of more flexible working arrangements from a variety of locations outside the typical nine-to-five business hours is here to stay – not necessarily on a daily basis, but in a way that allows people to be more productive and see direct benefits from technology.

Test and experiment

I've repeated time and again how digital revolves around people, and that includes your own communities. We all have our networks which can be found on just about every platform. There are Facebook groups covering every topic under the sun, LinkedIn connections and your own email list. These communities allow you to test and experiment with new ideas and gather feedback, in some cases before you've even created or launched a product or service.

Don't just treat communities as a potential customer pool, but engage with them. Listen and learn so they can inform your future direction and thinking to release products and services that add value in increasingly noisy marketplaces. The same goes for your clients and customers.

It's so frustrating to see discount offers land on the doormat or in your inbox with the small print that says 'Only valid for new customers'. I'm sure I can't be alone in thinking 'But I've been a customer for five years – where's my bonus?' Surprises and treats enhance people's experience of doing business with you, encouraging a sense of community in such a way that they talk about you positively, becoming ambassadors for your brand.

Make continual improvement the norm

Continual improvement in digital has to be the norm. Whether you're running ad campaigns, posting to Instagram or developing your website, constantly look at data, listen to your audience and analyse what works best. Marketing pioneer John Wanamaker who lived through the 1800s has been widely credited with the phrase, 'Half the money I spend on advertising is wasted; the trouble is I don't know which half.'[50] Today this is no such problem. Everything in digital can be measured, and marketing is becoming increasingly technical and scientific with possibilities to refine and optimise performance at every level to maximise your return on investment.

We talked about the idea of iterative design in the previous chapter, but it's only by listening and learning that you create progress and refine your customer offer. Customer experiences made up of ubiquitous access, convenience and ease of use are the new currency for loyalty, and a lack of dynamism stagnates your culture and growth as well as giving customers a reason to shop around. It's far less expensive to retain existing customers than it is to attract new ones, and people feel more loyalty when they benefit from a stream of continual improvement.

For your website, instead of going through a costly redesign every three years like so many other companies, allocate a predictable monthly budget to keeping your website optimised and performing at its best, rather than allowing it to become abandoned and ineffective. It's unlikely that the launch of a new

---

50 G Bradt, 'Wanamaker was wrong – the vast majority of advertising is wasted', *Forbes*, 2016, www.forbes.com/sites/georgebradt/ 2016/09/14/wanamaker-was-wrong-the-vast-majority-of-advertising-is-wasted

website will incorporate everything that was in your brief, so being able to determine how and where it's best to focus your effort over time allows you to make well-considered investments.

Set a consistent standard

As your new website goes out into the wild, it will look great. Art-directed images will have been carefully selected and perfectly aligned, and it will load quickly and be accessible across as many devices as possible. But if there's one thing that makes a web designer's heart sink, it's returning to the site in three months' time to find the love and attention given to it during the build stage has all but gone.

I get it. You've got a new CMS that gives you easy access to update your site. You're feeling empowered and full of enthusiasm to make the most of your new website and take the world by storm. But in your excitement, it's easy to take short cuts. Uploading a 10mb photo straight off a DSLR camera or choosing to quickly publish a PDF document rather than creating a new page can impact performance and data collection, and even carry a financial cost.

OK, perhaps I'm being a little unfair. Not everyone is a designer or has access to the latest version of Photoshop®, but housekeeping on your website is so important if you're going to see the results you discussed as the project started. There are plenty of low-cost tools for resizing and cropping images, although ideally these tools will be built into your CMS, making site administration and upkeep easier.

In truth, your website should prevent you making some of these mistakes. No one should be able to upload a 10mb photo, or if they can, it should at least be automatically scaled to an appropriate size and quality. But not everything can be automated and certain functionality may be restricted by your budget or limitations in your hosting environment. Choosing inappropriate stock images, typing in capitals or overlooking calls to action can all weaken the desired impact of your website.

For the largest of websites, a visual *style guide* or *pattern library* might be built alongside it. Sometimes this will extend to an entire *design system*, covering everything from written tone of voice to individual design components such as icons, buttons or typography.

Training helps, too. There should naturally be a comprehensive handover from those building your site to those who are responsible for managing it on a day-to-day basis. But training tends to focus on providing practical guidance to use your CMS. A style guide or design system is like having a set of brand guidelines specific to your website. These are published online so they're easy to access and share across internal terms, external partners and new starters joining the team.

Google, as you might expect for the size of the business, has produced an entire design system (https://material.io), as has Uber (https://brand.uber.com). Challenger bank Monzo has published its tone of voice guidelines (https://monzo.com/tone-of-voice) and Mailchimp's conversational tone is designed to empowered users without them feeling patronised (https://styleguide.mailchimp.com/voice-and-tone).

These are excellent examples of setting an expectation of what 'good' should look like from global businesses serving millions of customers worldwide, so for many companies, such a comprehensive approach won't be necessary. But you can see by looking at these examples how they enforce consistency, uphold brand standards and provide a platform for efficient development that doesn't keep reinventing the wheel.

Keep your technology current

It goes without saying that technology is constantly evolving, so you need to do all you can to keep pace with it. That's not to say you should be jumping into the latest shiny app available, but at least be aware of new tools that will support your processes, improve your data and encourage your cultural development.

Many of the cloud-based SaaS apps are constantly and quietly updating with new features (think continual development), and with most running in a web browser with no software to install, there's little responsibility in maintaining some of your core business software. Keeping your website platform up to date, however, will be crucial to patch vulnerabilities and safeguard your investment.

While some websites offer one-click or even automatic updates, more complex sites will require planning and testing prior to new releases being applied. Having a support contract for your website will enable you to ensure it's maintained regularly, reducing the gaps between releases, which generally makes for smoother upgrades with less chance of things going wrong during the process. It's a fact of life that bugs exist in software, so maintenance will minimise the risk of errors and reduce the likelihood of a vulnerability that could expose your website to hackers.

Data security is increasingly in the spotlight and it will only be a matter of time before the next major brand is thrust into the headlines as the result of a data breach. Not only is this enormously damaging to your brand, but as we discussed in the technology chapter, there are significant penalties for those who fail to adequately safeguard private data.

It's a marathon, not a sprint

Although we've talked extensively about sprints and their benefits, investing in digital is more of a marathon. Things don't happen overnight. It'll take time to plan them and put the right resources in place. There'll be experiments and mistakes, perhaps even growing pains, but the transition is vital to build a sustainable business that can achieve long-term success as we live through unprecedented change.

Wait, what about design?

We've reached the end of a book about planning your website and I hear you ask, 'Where's the section about design?' Well, I've been talking about design throughout the book.

American art director Paul Rand was quoted as saying, 'Design is the method of putting form and content together. Design, just as art, has multiple definitions, there is no single definition. Design can be art. Design can be aesthetics. Design is so simple, that's why it is so complicated.'[51]

Each step of the DISTANCE method raises questions about systems and service design and how this will impact on the overall experience faced by your users. People often rush to consider what a new website will look like over everything else because it's what people see that leaves them with a memorable first impression.

---

51 J Maeda, Interview: The original text, 1996, www.paulrand.design/life/interviews/2000-maeda-at-media.html

It's perfectly reasonable to like a particular visual style, or reference other websites when considering the visual design for your website. Your brand guidelines are important, as is using clear typography, an accessible colour scheme and flowing page layouts.

When you've considered each stage in my DISTANCE method, you will have everything you need to start thinking about how the website should look. This will be far more subjective than what data tells you, the facts about your audience or how you improve your internal process. This isn't a beauty parade; you need to know what will work for the site and how it will achieve its goals. If the goal is to win a design award, then clearly design becomes a much greater part of the conversation. However, I've never worked on a website for a business where people's appreciation of the design is the primary outcome.

Summary

Digital is wide ranging, but your website should be central to how you approach it. Your website captures and relays data, supports internal process and takes the lead in your strategy. Technology is all around us, but merely as a facilitator and enabler. People, whether in your target audience or team, will drive your culture with clear execution necessary to continually improve and adapt.

Websites needn't be complicated, but they do take a lot of work to pull together with an increasing number of moving parts supported by people across different teams and locations, often as a project over and above their day-to-day work. I hope as you've progressed through the book, you've learned how, with structured planning, you stand to achieve a successful website that becomes one of your business's strongest-performing assets.

Websites have in some cases become throwaway. There's nothing physical, and the words, photos and videos can always be used somewhere else. Maybe even in the next website. But this cycle has to be broken. Could you make your next website project your last? Perhaps not, but at least make your next website last longer than it might have done without a thorough plan to support it.

We're not quite done yet. In the final pages of this book, you'll find some useful resources, further reading and links to a number of online tools and platforms I'd recommend. I wish you all the best with your digital projects and hope the ideas in this book help you to formalise your thinking when planning a new website to deliver great results. Perhaps there'll be an opportunity for me to meet you at a live event or through an online workshop, but in the meantime, please do share the details of this book among your network and colleagues.

Actions

I'd love to hear from you, so please let me know what you thought of *Holistic Website Planning* by leaving a review at https://gothedistance.website/review or on amazon.co.uk. You could even take an Instagram selfie of you reading the book with the hashtag #gonethedistance, or reach me directly by email via andrew@gothedistance.website.

Alongside this book is a companion website at https://gothedistance.website. Here you'll find a selection of useful tools and resources that you can use in your own website projects. To benchmark your current digital performance and plan your strategy, including setting priorities on where to improve your digital marketing, please visit the online scorecard at https://gothedistance.website/score. This free tool will take you fewer than five minutes to complete and provide you with a personalised report on how you can start improving your digital marketing today. You can also benefit from a free thirty-minute call to talk through your results with me or my team at A Digital.

The Clientside Podcast is a regular podcast discussing all manner of digital topics with a range of guests from both inside and outside the digital space. Search for *The Clientside Podcast, Andrew Armitage* on any of the popular podcast apps, and if you enjoy the show, please like, subscribe, leave a review and share the details with your colleagues to help more people discover the resource.

Further Resources

A list of selected recommended reading, depending on your job role.

Birss, D *How to Get to Great Ideas: A system for smart, extraordinary thinking* (Nicholas Brealey, 2018)

Brown, T *Change by Design, Revised and Updated: How design thinking transforms organizations and inspires innovation* (HarperBus, 2019)

Hane, C; Atherton, M *Designing Connected Content: Plan and model digital products for tomorrow (Voices that matter)* (New Riders, 2018)

Hieatt, D *Do Purpose: Why brands with a purpose do better and matter more* (The Do Book Co, 2014)

Horwath, R *Elevate: The three disciplines of advanced strategic thinking* (Wiley, 2014)

Knapp, J *Sprint: How to solve big problems and test new ideas in just five days* (Simon Schuster, 2016)

Lewrick, M; Link, P; Leifer, L *The Design Thinking Playbook: Mindful digital transformation of teams, products, services, businesses and ecosystems* (Wiley, 2018)

Lichlaw, D *The User's Journey: Storymapping products that people love* (Rosenfeld Media, 2016)

McGovern, G *Top Tasks: A how-to guide* (Silver Beach, 2018)

McGovern, G *World Wide Waste: How digital is killing our planet. And what we can do about it* (Silver Beach, 2020)

Miller, D *Building a StoryBrand: Clarify your message so customers will listen* (Thomas Nelson, 2017)

Pine II, BJ; Gilmore, JH *The Experience Economy* (Harvard Business Review Press, 2011)

Priestley, D *Oversubscribed: How to get people lining up to do business with you* (Capstone, 2015)

Priestley, D *24 Assets: Create a digital, scalable, valuable and fun business that will thrive in a fast changing world* (Rethink Press, 2017)

Rowles, D; Brown, T *Building Digital Culture: A practical guide to successful digital transformation* (Kogan Page, 2020)

Sheridan, M *They Ask You Answer: A revolutionary approach to inbound sales, content marketing and today's digital consumer* (Wiley, 2017)

Williams, R *Non-Designer's Design Book* (Peachpit Press, 2014)

Here is a list of recommended tools that can be helpful at various stages of building or running a website:

Collaboration tools:

- Airtable – www.airtable.com

- Asana – www.asana.com

- Basecamp – www.basecamp.com

- ClickUp – www.clickup.com

- Jira – www.atlassian.com/software/jira

- Miro – www.miro.com

- Monday.com – www.monday.com

- Notion – www.notion.so

- Teamwork – www.teamwork.com

Graphics and video:

- Adobe Creative Cloud – www.adobe.com

- Canva – www.canva.com

- Lightworks (PC) – www.lwks.com

- Screenflow Pro (Mac) – www.macupdate.com/app/mac/26915/screenflow

Content planning, site-mapping and auditing:

- ContentCal – www.contentcal.io

- GatherContent – www.gathercontent.com

- Raven Tools – www.raventools.com

- Semrush – www.semrush.com

- Slickplan – www.slickplan.com

Podcast hosting:

- Anchor (free!) – www.anchor.fm

- Podcast.co – www.podcast.co

File sharing:

- Dropbox – www.dropbox.com

- Google Drive – www.google.com/intl/en_jm/drive

- SmugMug – www.smugmug.com

Website CMSs:

- Craft CMS – www.craftcms.com
- Statamic – www.statamic.com

Usability testing:

- Userbrain – www.userbrain.net
- UserTesting – www.usertesting.com
- Maze – https://maze.co

Analytics tools:

- FullStory – www.fullstory.com
- Hotjar – www.hotjar.com

Acknowledgements

The planning, writing and editing of this book has taken place over almost two years, and while I may be the credited author, there are plenty of people who have supported me throughout the process of not only writing the book, but also running and building my own business.

Firstly, I would like to thank my amazing wife Louise and our two wonderful daughters Sophie and Ellie for your ever-present support and encouragement. Thank you for your patience with the early starts and late finishes. For much of the writing process, I've been accompanied by Bentley, our flat-coated retriever, who didn't provide much by way of words, but was always there to listen to my thinking. I love you all.

I would like to thank my family who have always been there to support me throughout my business journey. Dad, you were my inspiration to start my own business and provided for us as Katie and I grew up together. Mum, you have always encouraged us to pursue our own paths with love and support that know no bounds. To my in-laws Chris and Mike who have always been supportive and helped to entertain the kids on many an occasion to allow work to happen.

I'd like to thank clients past and present for trusting my team and me with your digital strategies and website projects. It's humbling to see our work supporting your own business journeys, contributing to job creation and causes, and it's been a privilege to have been a part of that. By extension, thank you to the team at A Digital for your tenacity throughout the pandemic and desire to see the business grow by providing a positive and successful experience for our clients.

Thank you to those who have provided the tools and frameworks, some of which are referenced in this book, that help us to shape and formalise creative ideas. Building websites is a collaborative process, and the digital industry has always been incredibly open and generous in sharing ideas and best practice. It's a fantastic sector to work in and I've met some amazing people along the way who are too numerous to mention. You'll know who you are.

Thank you also to my peer group: Jonathan Hemus, Sophie Milliken, Simon Shepherd and Paul Turner. Your ongoing support and encouragement as confidantes has been hugely appreciated and I very much value the friendships we've built.

I also want to thank Daniel Priestley and members of the global Dent community for your inspiration, insight and regular reminders of what can be achieved when you focus your mind to something, sharing your wins and your challenges.

Finally, thank you to the team at Rethink Press for your guidance throughout the editing and publishing process.

The Author

Andrew Armitage is the founder and director of multi-award-winning digital agency A Digital. With over twenty years' experience working on digital projects for companies including ExxonMobil and the NHS, leading visitor attraction Windermere Lake Cruises and renowned paper manufacturer James Cropper plc, Andrew has seen and worked on website projects of all sizes. He has also been a consultant for Winning Moves, delivering funded digital programmes to SME businesses across Cumbria.

A Digital typically works with B2B clients in professional services, tourism and hospitality, manufacturing, food and drink, and both B2B and B2C eCommerce. Andrew's passion is demonstrating the benefits technology can bring to businesses with great design and sharing his knowledge so others can raise their digital game to drive business growth in the modern economy. He's spoken at conferences internationally and hosts a podcast called *The Clientside* which can be found on all popular podcast apps.

Andrew lives with his wife, two young daughters and their flat-coated retriever Bentley on the edge of the Lake District in north-west England. A keen outdoor enthusiast, Andrew will often be found spending time walking in the Lakes with his family or riding the off-road trails on his mountain bike.

Social media links:

- www.linkedin.com/in/andrewarmitage
- https://twitter.com/aarmitage
- https://instagram.com/aarmitage
- www.youtube.com/channel/UCiA-ux4-xkG4eRqc738e_yA

Additional links:

Digital Agency: https://adigital.agency

Podcast: https://theclientside.show

Companion Website: https://gothedistance.website

Online Scorecard: https://gothedistance.website/score

Public Facebook Group: www.facebook.com/groups/clientsidedigitalcommunity

Printed in Great Britain
by Amazon

78820761R00159